Review, Practice, & Mastery of

COMMON CORE
ENGLISH LANGUAGE ARTS
STATE STANDARDS

Reviewers
Amy Barr • Park Hill School District • Park Hill, MO
Tracie Baumgartner • Valley View School District • Bolingbrook, IL
Barbara Burns • Lammersville Unified School District • Mountain House, CA
Jane Carlton • North Marion School District • Aurora, OR
Karen Cooke • Cobb County School District • Marietta, GA
Amy Corr • Douglas County School District • Highlands Ranch, CO
Rachel Nichols • Lower Merion School District • Ardmore, PA
Arlene Peters • Orange County Public Schools • Orlando, FL
Debbie Romo • Union School District • Tulsa, OK
Brian Selling • Community Day Charter School • Lawrence, MA
Kim Sheehy • Sauquoit Valley Central Schools • Sauquoit, NY
Beverly Smith • Corona-Norco Unified School District • Ontario, CA
Colleen Thomas • Sandwich Public Schools • Sandwich, MA
Holly Walker • Whitman-Hanson Regional School District • Hanson, MA

© 2015 **Perfection Learning®**

Please visit our Web site at:
www.perfectionlearning.com

When ordering this book, please specify:
ISBN-13: 978-0-7891-8933-2 or **14869**

1 2 3 4 5 6 PP 19 18 17 16 15

Printed in the United States of America

To the Student

This book will help you review, practice, and master the English Language Arts Common Core State Standards. Here are the steps to follow to use this book.

1. Take the Tryout Test over Reading Literature, Reading Informational Text, and Language. Then check your answers. Use the chart below to find out your strengths and weaknesses in the areas covered. Remember the questions that are hard for you to answer. These will be the types of questions you need to work on the most.

2. Work through the units that follow the Tryout Test. The lessons in each unit review example items and provide a practice test based on the standards. Fill in the Keeping Score chart on page 161 as you complete each practice test.

3. After completing all the lessons, take the Mastery Test. Your score on this test will show your understanding of the Common Core Standards.

4. Work through the Writing Test Workshop section of the book. These lessons will help you learn how to read a writing prompt and how to get your ideas down on paper in a clear and organized manner.

Reading Literature	Tryout Test Items	Mastery Test Items
Unit One—Key Ideas and Details		
Lesson 1 Cite, Infer, and Summarize	8, 15, 20	11
Lesson 2 Character and Theme	1, 2, 3, 17	1, 2, 3, 8, 9, 15, 17
Unit Two—Craft and Structure		
Lesson 3 Word Choice	4, 5, 6, 10, 16	5, 6, 10, 12, 14
Lesson 4 Structure	11, 12, 13	13
Lesson 5 Point of View	14	7
Reading Informational Text	Tryout Test Items	Mastery Test Items
Unit Three—Key Ideas and Details		
Lesson 6 Cite, Infer, and Summarize	21, 22, 26, 31	19, 27, 31, 32, 33, 34, 35
Lesson 7 Supporting Details	25, 28, 29, 38	21, 37
Unit Four—Craft and Structure		
Lesson 8 Word Choice	35	4, 23
Lesson 9 Structure and Point of View	23, 24, 32, 37	18, 20, 22
Unit Five—Integration of Knowledge and Ideas		
Lesson 10 Arguments and Claims	27, 33, 36	29, 36
Lesson 11 U.S. Documents	30, 34	28, 30
Language	Tryout Test Items	Mastery Test Items
Unit Six—Conventions of Standard English		
Lesson 12 Grammar and Usage	39, 40, 41, 42, 43, 50	38, 39, 40, 41, 42, 43, 44
Lesson 13 Punctuation and Spelling	44, 45, 46, 47, 48, 49	45, 46, 47, 48, 49, 50
Unit Seven—Vocabulary		
Lesson 14 Context Clues and Reference Materials	7, 18, 19	25, 26
Lesson 15 Word Patterns and Relationships	9	16, 24

Common Core
Grade
9

Table of Contents

Reading Literature

Unit One—Key Ideas and Details

Unit Two—Craft and Structure

continued

Reading Informational Text

Unit Three—Key Ideas and Details

continued

Table of Contents continued

Unit Four—Craft and Structure

Unit Five—Integration of Knowledge and Ideas

Language

Unit Six—Conventions of Standard English

continued

continued

Table of Contents continued

Writing

Standards Key: RL = Reading Literature, RI = Reading Informational Text,
L = Language, W = Writing, RH = Reading Standards for Literacy in History/Social Studies,
RST = Reading Standards for Literacy in Science/Technical Studies, WHST = Writing Standards
for Literacy in History/Social Studies, Science, and Technical Subjects

Note: A complete correlation of the Grade 9 Common Core State Standards for English Langauge
Arts can be found in the Grade 9 Teacher Guide.

Tryout Test: Part 1

Estimated time: 50 minutes

Directions: Read the passage and answer the questions that follow.

The Gift of the Magi

by O. Henry

1 "Jim, darling," she cried, "don't look at me that way. I had my hair cut off and sold because I couldn't have lived through Christmas without giving you a present. It'll grow out again--you won't mind, will you? I just had to do it. My hair grows awfully fast. Say 'Merry Christmas!' Jim, and let's be happy. You don't know what a nice—what a beautiful, nice gift I've got for you."

2 "You've cut off your hair?" asked Jim, laboriously, as if he had not arrived at that patent fact yet even after the hardest mental labor.

3 "Cut it off and sold it," said Della. "Don't you like me just as well, anyhow? I'm me without my hair, ain't I?"

4 Jim looked about the room curiously.

5 "You say your hair is gone?" he said, with an air almost of idiocy.

6 "You needn't look for it," said Della. "It's sold, I tell you—sold and gone, too. It's Christmas Eve, boy. Be good to me, for it went for you. Maybe the hairs of my head were numbered," she went on with sudden serious sweetness, "but nobody could ever count my love for you. Shall I put the chops on, Jim?"

7 Out of his trance Jim seemed quickly to wake. He enfolded his Della. For ten seconds let us regard with discreet scrutiny some inconsequential object in the other direction. Eight dollars a week or a million a year—what is the difference? A mathematician or a wit would give you the wrong answer. The magi brought valuable gifts, but that was not among them. This dark assertion will be illuminated later on.

8 Jim drew a package from his overcoat pocket and threw it upon the table."Don't make any mistake, Dell," he said, "about me. I don't think there's anything in the way of a haircut or a shave or a shampoo that could make me like my girl any less. But if you'll unwrap that package you may see why you had me going a while at first."

9 White fingers and nimble tore at the string and paper. And then an ecstatic scream of joy; and then, alas! a quick feminine change to hysterical tears and wails, necessitating the immediate employment of all the comforting powers of the lord of the flat.

10 For there lay The Combs—the set of combs, side and back, that Della had worshipped long in a Broadway window. Beautiful combs, pure tortoise shell, with jewelled rims—just the shade to wear in the beautiful vanished hair. They were expensive combs, she knew, and her heart had simply craved and yearned over them without the least hope of possession. And now, they were hers, but the tresses that should have adorned the coveted adornments were gone.

11 But she hugged them to her bosom, and at length she was able to look up with dim eyes and a smile and say: "My hair grows so fast, Jim!"

12 And then Della leaped up like a little singed cat and cried, "Oh, oh!"

13   Jim had not yet seen his beautiful present. She held it out to him eagerly upon her open palm. The dull precious metal seemed to flash with a reflection of her bright and ardent spirit.

14   "Isn't it a dandy, Jim? I hunted all over town to find it. You'll have to look at the time a hundred times a day now. Give me your watch. I want to see how it looks on it."

15   Instead of obeying, Jim tumbled down on the couch and put his hands under the back of his head and smiled.

16   "Dell," said he, "let's put our Christmas presents away and keep 'em a while. They're too nice to use just at present. I sold the watch to get the money to buy your combs. And now suppose you put the chops on."

17   The magi, as you know, were wise men—wonderfully wise men—who brought gifts to the Babe in the manger. They invented the art of giving Christmas presents. Being wise, their gifts were no doubt wise ones, possibly bearing the privilege of exchange in case of duplication. And here I have lamely related to you the uneventful <u>chronicle</u> of two foolish children in a flat who most unwisely sacrificed for each other the greatest treasures of their house. But in a last word to the wise of these days let it be said that of all who give gifts these two were the wisest. Of all who give and receive gifts, such as they are wisest. Everywhere they are wisest. They are the magi.

---

1   What theme is revealed in the passage?

   A Love is blind.

   B Love is the best gift.

   C Love is foolish.

   D Love is a strange feeling.

2   Which paragraph from the passage best shows this same theme?

   A paragraph 6

   B paragraph 9

   C paragraph 14

   D paragraph 17

3   What traditional character is Della most like?

   A a damsel in distress

   B a mean witch

   C an evil stepmother

   D a kind princess

4 Read this excerpt from the passage.

> And then Della leaped up like a little singed cat...

The author compares Della to a cat in order to—

A show how quickly she moved.

B draw attention to how small Della is.

C suggest that Della is animal-like.

D create the idea that Della is a cat.

5 What is the meaning of the word <u>chronicle</u> as it is used in the last paragraph?

A memory

B explanation

C reflection

D story

6 Which of the details from the excerpt helps the reader understand the meaning of <u>chronicle</u>?

A *And here I have lamely related to you . . .*

B *. . . who most unwisely sacrificed for each other . . .*

C *. . .the greatest treasures of their house.*

D *. . . in a last word to the wise of these days . . .*

7 The author's choice of words in the last paragraph helps the story end—

A on an uplifting note.

B with suspense.

C with a surprise twist in the plot.

D on a sad note.

8 Write a summary of the story. Include only the main events. (3 points)

_____

_____

_____

_____

_____

_____

Directions: Read the poem and answer the questions that follow.

Song

by John Donne

Goe, and catche a falling starre,
   Get with child a mandrake roote,
Tell me, where all past yeares are,
   Or who cleft the Divel's foot,
Teach me to heare Mermaides singing,
   Or to keep off envies stinging,
And finde
   What winde
Serves to advance an honest minde.

If thou beest borne to strange sights,
   Things invisible to see,
Ride ten thousand daies and nights,
   Till age snow white haires on thee,

Thou, when thou return'st, wilt tell mee
   All strange wonders that befell thee,
And sweare
   No where
Lives a woman true, and faire.

If thou findst one, let mee know,
   Such a Pilgrimage were sweet;
Yet doe not, I would not goe,
   Though at next doore wee might meet,
Though shee were true, when you met her,
   And last, till you write your letter,
Yet shee
   Will bee
False, ere I come, to two, or three.

---

9 Finish the following word analogy.

STAR : SKY :: Mermaid :

A creature

B lady

C myth

D sea

10 The poet uses words such as *strange, invisible,* and *false* to create a tone of—

A suspicion.

B jealousy.

C astonishment.

D amazement.

11 The first stanza of the poem—

    A introduces the characters.

    B describes impossible things.

    C gives away the ending.

    D explains the setting.

12 What impact does using poetry to describe finding a "true and faire" woman have on readers?

    A The words present a true account of how one man searched for love.

    B The language shows how difficult travel was during that time period.

    C Poetry appeals to readers because it is usually divided into stanzas and is easy to read.

    D The words and images of the poem appeal to readers' emotions.

13 How are the structures of "The Gift of the Magi" and "Song" different? How do their different structures communicate the meaning of each work? Use textual evidence in the form of quotations and examples from BOTH passages to support your answer. (3 points)

_____

_____

_____

_____

_____

_____

_____

_____

_____

_____

_____

_____

_____

_____

Directions: Read the passage and answer the questions that follow.

from The Bonesetter's Daughter

by Amy Tan

I was sleepy, still lying on the brick k'ang bed I shared with Precious Auntie. The flue to our little room was furthest from the stove in the common room, and the bricks beneath me had long turned cold. I felt my shoulder being shaken. When I opened my eyes, Precious Auntie began to write on a scrap of paper, then showed me what she had written. "I can't see," I complained. "It's too dark."

She huffed, set the paper on the low cupboard, and motioned that I should get up. She lighted the teapot brazier, and tied a scarf over her nose and mouth when it started to smoke. She poured face-washing water into the teapot's chamber, and when it was cooked, she started our day. She scrubbed my face and ears. She parted my hair and combed my bangs. She wet down any strands that stuck out like spider legs. Then she gathered the long part of my hair into two bundles and braided them. She banded the top with red ribbon, the bottom with green. I wagged my head so that my braids swung like the happy ears of palace dogs. And Precious Auntie sniffed the air as if she, too, were a dog wondering, What's that good smell? That sniff was how she said my nickname, Doggie. That was how she talked.

She had no voice, just gasps and wheezes, the snorts of a ragged wind. She told me things with grimaces and groans, dancing eyebrows and darting eyes. She wrote about the world on my carry-around chalkboard. She also made pictures with her blackened hands. Hand-talk, face-talk, and chalk-talk were the languages I grew up with, soundless and strong.

As she wound her hair tight against her skull, I played with her box of treasures. I took out a pretty comb, ivory with a rooster carved at each end. Precious Auntie was born a Rooster. "You wear this," I demanded, holding it up. "Pretty." I was still young enough to believe that beauty came from things, and I wanted Mother to favor her more. But Precious Auntie shook her head. She pulled off her scarf and pointed to her face and bunched her eyebrows. What use do I have for prettiness? she was saying.

Her bangs fell to her eyebrows like mine. The rest of her hair was bound into a knot and stabbed together with a silver prong. She had a sweet-peach forehead, wide-set eyes, full cheeks tapering to a small plump nose. That was the top of her face. Then there was the bottom.

She wiggled blackened fingertips like hungry flames. See what the fire did.

I didn't think she was ugly, not in the way others in our family did. "Ai-ya, seeing her, even a demon would leap out of his skin," I once heard Mother remark. When I was small, I liked to trace my fingers around Precious Auntie's mouth. It was a puzzle. Half was bumpy, half was smooth and melted closed. The inside of her right cheek was stiff as leather, the left was moist and soft. Where the gums had burned, the teeth had fallen out. And her tongue was like a parched root. She could not taste the pleasures of life: salty and bitter, sour and sharp, spicy, sweet, and fat.

No one else understood Precious Auntie's kind of talk, so I had to say aloud what she meant. Not everything, though, not our secret stories. She often told me about her father, the Famous Bonesetter from the Mouth of the

Mountain, about the cave where they found the dragon bones, how the bones were divine and could cure any pain, except a grieving heart. "Tell me again," I said that morning, wishing for a story about how she burned her face and became my nursemaid.

I was a fire-eater, she said with her hands and eyes. Hundreds of people came to see me in the market square. Into the burning pot of my mouth I dropped raw pork, added chilis and bean paste, stirred this up, then offered the morsels to people to taste. If they said, "Delicious!" I opened my mouth as a purse to catch their copper coins. One day, however, I ate the fire, and the fire came back, and it ate me. After that, I decided not to be a cook-pot anymore, so I became your nursemaid instead.

I laughed and clapped my hands, liking this made-up story best. The day before, she told me she had stared at an unlucky star falling out of the sky and then it dropped into her open mouth and burned her face. The day before that, she said she had eaten what she thought was a spicy Hunan dish only to find that it was the coals used for cooking.

14 How does the author use the narrator's point of view to create suspense? Use direct quotes and explanations examples from the passage to support your answer. (3 points)

_____

_____

_____

_____

_____

_____

_____

_____

_____

_____

_____

_____

_____

15 What detail from the story helps you infer that the narrator realized that other people were unkind to Precious Auntie?

   A The narrator is the only one who can understand Precious Auntie's stories.

   B The narrator does not think Precious Auntie is ugly the way other family members do.

   C The narrator knows that Precious Auntie cannot taste different flavors.

   D Precious Auntie was the daughter of the Famous Bonesetter.

16 The phrase "my braids swung like the happy ears of palace dogs" means—

   A the braids swayed to and fro.

   B the braids were smooth and silky.

   C dogs like to play with braids.

   D palace dogs are usually happy.

17 Why does the narrator ask Precious Auntie for a story?

   A She knows no one else listens to Precious Auntie.

   B She wants to tell a new story at school.

   C She likes to hear the imaginative tales.

   D She wants her mother to like Precious Auntie more.

18 Use this sample dictionary entry for the word *favor* to answer the question.

> **fa•vor** (fey vər) [Latin *favōr-*] v. **1.** To show someone preferential treatment. **2.** To help someone. **3.** To be careful with something. **4.** To resemble someone.

Which definition best fits *favor* as it is used in paragraph 4?

   A definition 1

   B definition 2

   C definition 3

   D definition 4

19 Which part of the dictionary entry explains the origin of the word?

   A favor

   B (fey-vər)

   C [Latin *favōr-*]

   D v.

GO ON

20 How do Precious Auntie's actions in the passage show what she is like? Use evidence from the story to explain Precious Auntie's character. (5 points)

_____

_____

_____

_____

_____

_____

_____

_____

_____

_____

_____

_____

_____

_____

Take a break. Then go on to Part 2.

Directions: Read the passage and answer the questions that follow.

from The Basque History of the World

by Mark Kurlansky

The central mystery is: Who are the Basques? The early Basques left no written records, and the first accounts of them, two centuries after the Romans arrived in 218 B.C., give the impression that they were already an ancient—or at least not a new people. Artifacts predating this time that have been found in the area—a few tools, drawings in caves, and the rudiments of ruins—cannot be proved to have been made by the Basques, though it is supposed that at least some of them were.

Ample evidence exists that the Basques are a physically distinct group. There is a Basque type with a long straight nose, thick eyebrows, strong chin, and long earlobes. Even today, sitting in a bar in a mountainous river valley town like Tolosa, watching men play mus, the popular card game, one can see a similarity in the faces, despite considerable intermarriage. Personalities, of course, carve very different visages, but over and over again, from behind a hand of cards, the same eyebrows, chin, and nose can be seen. The identical dark navy wool berets so many men wear—each in a slightly different manner—seem to showcase the long Basque ears sticking out on the sides. In past eras, when Spaniards and French were typically fairly small people, Basque men were characteristically larger, thick chested, broad shouldered, and burly. Because these were also characteristics of Cro-Magnons, Basques are often thought to be direct descendants of this man who lived 40,000 years ago.

Less subjective physical evidence of an ancient and distinct group has also surfaced. In the beginning of the twentieth century, it was discovered that all blood was one of three types: A, B, or O. Basques have the highest concentration of type O in the world—more than 50 percent of the population—with an even higher percentage in remote areas where the language is best preserved, such as Soule. Most of the rest are type A. Type B is extremely rare among Basques. With the finding that Irish, Scots, Corsicans, and Cretans also have an unusually high incidence of type O, speculation ran wild that these peoples were somehow related to the Basques. But then, in 1937, came the discovery of the rhesus factor; more commonly known as Rh-positive or Rh-negative. Basques were found to have the highest incidences of Rh-negative blood of any people in the world, significantly higher than the rest of Europe, even significantly higher than neighboring regions of France and Spain. Cro-Magnon theorists point out that other places known to have been occupied by Cro-Magnon man, such as the Atlas Mountains of Morocco and the Canary Islands, also have been found to have a high incidence of Rh-negative.

Twenty-seven percent of Basques have O Rh-negative blood. Rh-negative blood in a pregnant woman can fatally poison a fetus that has positive blood. Since World War II,

GO ON

intervention techniques to save the fetus have been developed, but it is probable that throughout history, the rate of miscarriage and stillborn births among the Basque was extremely high, which may be one of the reasons they remained a small population on a limited amount of land while other populations, especially in Iberia, grew rapidly.

Before Basque blood was studied as a key to their origins, several attempts were made to analyze the structure of Basque skulls. At the beginning of the nineteenth century, a researcher reported, "Someone gave me a Basque body and I dissected it and I assert that the head was not built like that of other men."

Studies of Basque skulls in the nineteenth century concluded, depending on whose study is believed, that Basques were either Turks, Tartars, Magyars, Germans, Laplanders, or the descendants of Cro-Magnon man either originating in Basqueland or coming from the Berbers of North Africa.

Or do clothes hold the secret to Basque origins? A twelfth-century writer, Aimeric de Picaud, considered not skulls but skirts, concluding after seeing Basque men in short ones that they were clearly descendants of Scots.

The most useful artifact left behind by the ancient Basques is their language. Linguists find that while the language has adopted foreign words, the grammar has proved resistant to change, so that modern Euskera is thought to be far closer to its ancient form than modern Greek is to ancient Greek. Euskera has extremely complex verbs and twelve cases, few forms of politeness, a limited number of abstractions, a rich vocabulary for natural phenomena, and no prepositions or articles.

Euskera Words and Their English Equivalents	
Euskera Word	**Translation**
Etxea	To the house
Etxean	At home
Etxetik	From home
Iparsortalderatu	To head in a northeasterly direction
Aitzur	Hoe
Aizkora	Axe
Aizto	Knife

21 Which sentence best summarizes the information in paragraphs 5 and 6?

   A Many have come up with various theories about Basque origins by studying skulls.

   B In the nineteenth century, many believed that Basques were Turks, Tartars, Magyars, and so on.

   C After dissecting a Basque body, a researcher claimed that it was different from that of other men.

   D The key to understanding the Basques lies in understanding the structure of their skulls.

22 What can you infer from reading this passage?

   A The Basques have a high incidence of O Rh-negative blood.

   B The Basques are an interesting subject of study for many researchers.

   C Modern Euskera is a dying language.

   D It is difficult to determine how long the Basque people have been around.

23 What is the purpose of the chart that accompanies this passage?

   A It describes how much more difficult it is to learn Euskera than it is to learn English.

   B It tells how English has more words than Euskera does.

   C It shows how one Euskera word can have the same meaning as several English words.

   D It lists unusual words in the Euskera language.

24 The author describes Euskera as having "no prepositions or articles." According to information in the chart, a Euskera word such as *etxea* changes its form slightly to—

   A imply the meaning of prepositions and articles found as separate words in English.

   B show that language does not require the use of prepositions and articles.

   C show how Euskera is a complicated language.

   D imply that prepositions and articles are the most important parts of Euskera.

25 What effect did having a high incidence of O Rh-negative blood have on the Basque people?

   A It made them appreciate children.

   B It made them aware that they were different from the rest of Europe.

   C It kept them from seeking medical help with pregnancy.

   D It kept their population small.

26 The author wrote this passage mainly to—

   A present facts and figures about the Basques.

   B describe the way blood type has affected the Basques.

   C explain the mystery surrounding the Basques.

   D encourage the reader to study the Basques.

27 The author believes that the Basques are a distinct group of people. Does the author provide sufficient evidence to support this viewpoint? Is the evidence relevant or does he include unrelated details? Use details and examples from the passage to support your answer. (3 points)

_____

_____

_____

_____

_____

_____

_____

_____

_____

_____

_____

_____

_____

_____

_____

_____

Directions: Read the passage and answer the questions that follow.

from Mission to Mars: My Vision for Space Exploration

by Buzz Aldrin

I know firsthand that challenging times often come first before the most rewarding moments. Over the centuries we have seen powerful reminders of those who explored beyond the boundaries of what they knew, from Copernicus and Galileo to Columbus. Jumping to the twentieth century, it was on a windswept morning in 1903 at Kitty Hawk that the Wright brothers made the first powered flight. That same year, my mother, Marion Moon, was born.

My father, Edwin Eugene Aldrin, was an engineer and an aviation pioneer—and a friend of Charles Lindbergh and Orville Wright. Taking a job with Standard Oil, my dad flew his own plane coast to coast. He later served in World War II in the Army Air Corps, coming home for visits.

Born in 1930 and raised in Montclair, New Jersey, I finished high school there. Aviation was pretty much in the family. When I was all of two years of age, my dad took me on my first flight, the two of us winging our way from Newark down to Miami to visit relatives. My aunt, in fact, was a stewardess for Eastern Airlines. The Lockheed Vega single-engine plane that I flew in was trimmed in red paint to look like an eagle. How could I have grasped then as a child that decades later I would find myself strapped inside a very different breed of flying machine—Apollo 11's lander, the *Eagle*, en route to the moon's Sea of Tranquility?

The heritage that led me into aviation and the appreciation for higher education came from my father. Dad had gone to Clark University in Worcester, Massachusetts. His physics professor was Robert Goddard, regarded as the father of liquid-fueled rocketry.

After graduation from high school, I became a cadet at West Point and took to heart its motto, "Duty, Honor, Country." It's a maxim that remains part of me today. Surrounded by the influence of aviation, I entered the U.S. Air Force after graduating from the Military Academy. After fighter pilot training I was stationed in Korea, where I flew 66 combat missions in my F-86 Sabre fighter jet, shooting down two enemy MiG-15 aircraft.

Following the Korean War, I was sent to Germany and was on alert, flying F-100s that carried nuclear weapons. In the late 1950s the Cold War was escalating between the then Soviet Union and the United States. To be sure, tensions were high. While posted in Germany, I learned of the Soviets' surprising technological feat—the launch of Earth's first artificial satellite in October 1957, a 184-pound sphere called *Sputnik*. As the import of *Sputnik* sank in, against the backdrop of the Cold War, the political and public reaction spurred on the space age. It became the starting gun for the space race, leading to the creation of NASA the following year.

GO ON

The Soviet Union achieved yet another triumph on April 12, 1961, by sending the first human into Earth orbit, cosmonaut Yuri Gagarin, in his *Vostok* 1 spacecraft. As a comparative note, a few weeks after Gagarin's mission of 108 minutes duration, NASA flew on May 5 America's first Mercury astronaut, Alan Shepard, on a 15-minute suborbital flight that touched the edge of space.

A mere 20 days after Shepard's mission, President John F. Kennedy boldly challenged America to commit itself to achieving the goal of landing a man on the moon before the end of that decade. Many of those at the helm of a newly formed NASA thought the challenge to be impossible. The know-how just wasn't there. The nation had little more than 15 minutes of spaceflight experience under its belt.

But what America did have was a President with vision, determination, and the confidence that such a goal was attainable. By publicly stating our goal and by establishing an explicit time period on a very clear accomplishment, President Kennedy offered no back door. We either had to do it or not make the grade . . . and no one was interested in failing. Even then, failure was not an option.

Kennedy's audacious objective was further reinforced by his speech at Rice University on September 12, 1962. That seminal speech included the famed line: "We choose to go to the moon in this decade and do the other things, not because they are easy, but because they are hard." That presentation, even today, remains riveting.

28 When was *Sputnik* launched?

    A October 1957

    B April 1961

    C May 1961

    D September 1962

29 Which detail supports the idea that the Soviet Union's achievements motivated America to enter space?

    A The U.S. created NASA a year after the Soviets launched Sputnik.

    B Sputnik was a 184-pound sphere launched into space.

    C Yuri Gagarin became the first human to be launched into space.

    D Alan Shepard's flight touched the edge of space in 1961.

30 How does the writer use an important historical document to help explain a key idea about Americans going into space? Use examples from the passage to support your answer. (3 points)

_____

_____

_____

_____

_____

_____

_____

_____

_____

_____

_____

_____

_____

_____

_____

from **Kennedy's Speech to Rice University: The Decision to Go to the Moon**

by John F. Kennedy

We set sail on this new sea because there is new knowledge to be gained, and new rights to be won, and they must be won and used for the progress of all people. For space science, like nuclear science and all technology, has no conscience of its own. Whether it will become a force for good or ill depends on man, and only if the United States occupies a position of pre-eminence can we help decide whether this new ocean will be a sea of peace or a new terrifying theater of war. I do not say that we should or will go unprotected against the hostile misuse of space any more than we go unprotected against the hostile use of land or sea, but I do say that space can be explored and mastered without feeding the fires of war, without repeating the mistakes that man has made in extending his writ around this globe of ours.

There is no strife, no prejudice, no national conflict in outer space as yet. Its hazards are hostile to us all. Its conquest deserves the best of all mankind, and its opportunity for peaceful cooperation many never come again. But why, some say, the moon? Why choose this as our goal? And they may well ask why climb the highest mountain? Why, 35 years ago, fly the Atlantic? Why does Rice play Texas?

We choose to go to the moon. We choose to go to the moon in this decade and do the

GO ON

other things, not because they are easy, but because they are hard, because that goal will serve to organize and measure the best of our energies and skills, because that challenge is one that we are willing to accept, one we are unwilling to postpone, and one which we intend to win, and the others, too.

It is for these reasons that I regard the decision last year to shift our efforts in space from low to high gear as among the most important decisions that will be made during my incumbency in the office of the Presidency.

In the last 24 hours we have seen facilities now being created for the greatest and most complex exploration in man's history. We have felt the ground shake and the air shattered by the testing of a *Saturn C-1* booster rocket, many times as powerful as the *Atlas* which launched John Glenn, generating power equivalent to 10,000 automobiles with their accelerators on the floor. We have seen the site where five F-1 rocket engines, each one as powerful as all eight engines of the *Saturn* combined, will be clustered together to make the advanced *Saturn* missile, assembled in a new building to be built at Cape Canaveral as tall as a 48-story structure, as wide as a city block, and as long as two lengths of this field.

Within these last 19 months at least 45 satellites have circled the Earth. Some 40 of them were "made in the United States of America" and they were far more sophisticated and supplied far more knowledge to the people of the world than those of the Soviet Union.

The *Mariner* spacecraft now on its way to Venus is the most intricate instrument in the history of space science. The accuracy of that shot is comparable to firing a missile from Cape Canaveral and dropping it in this stadium between the 40-yard lines.

Transit satellites are helping our ships at sea to steer a safer course. Tiros satellites have given us unprecedented warnings of hurricanes and storms, and will do the same for forest fires and icebergs.

We have had our failures, but so have others, even if they do not admit them. And they may be less public.

To be sure, we are behind, and will be behind for some time in manned flight. But we do not intend to stay behind, and in this decade, we shall make up and move ahead.

The growth of our science and education will be enriched by new knowledge of our universe and environment, by new techniques of learning and mapping and observation, by new tools and computers for industry, medicine, the home as well as the school. Technical institutions, such as Rice, will reap the harvest of these gains.

And finally, the space effort itself, while still in its infancy, has already created a great number of new companies, and tens of thousands of new jobs. Space and related industries are generating new demands in investment and skilled personnel, and this city and this State, and this region, will share greatly in this growth. What was once the furthest outpost on the old frontier of the West will be the furthest outpost on the new frontier of science and space. Houston, your City of Houston, with its Manned Spacecraft Center, will become the heart of a large scientific and engineering community. During the next 5 years the National Aeronautics and Space Administration expects to double the number of scientists and engineers in this area, to increase its outlays for salaries and expenses to $60 million a year; to invest some $200 million in plant and laboratory facilities; and to direct or contract for new space efforts over $1 billion from this Center in this City.

To be sure, all this costs us all a good deal of money. This year's space budget is three times what it was in January 1961, and it is greater than the space budget of the previous eight years combined. That budget now stands at $5,400 million a year—a staggering sum, though somewhat less than we pay for cigarettes and cigars every year. Space expenditures will soon rise some more, from 40 cents per person per week to more than 50 cents a week for every man, woman and child in the United States, for we have given this program a high national priority—even though I realize that this is in some measure an act of faith and vision, for we do not now know what benefits await us. But if I were to say, my fellow citizens, that we shall send to the moon, 240,000 miles away from the control station in Houston, a giant rocket more than 300 feet tall, the length of this football field, made of new metal alloys, some of which have not yet been invented, capable of standing heat and stresses several times more than have ever been experienced, fitted together with a precision better than the finest watch, carrying all the equipment needed for propulsion, guidance, control, communications, food and survival, on an untried mission, to an unknown celestial body, and then return it safely to earth, re-entering the atmosphere at speeds of over 25,000 miles per hour, causing heat about half that of the temperature of the sun—

almost as hot as it is here today—and do all this, and do it right, and do it first before this decade is out—then we must be bold.

I'm the one who is doing all the work, so we just want you to stay cool for a minute. [laughter]

However, I think we're going to do it, and I think that we must pay what needs to be paid. I don't think we ought to waste any money, but I think we ought to do the job. And this will be done in the decade of the sixties. It may be done while some of you are still here at school at this college and university. It will be done during the term of office of some of the people who sit here on this platform. But it will be done. And it will be done before the end of this decade.

I am delighted that this university is playing a part in putting a man on the moon as part of a great national effort of the United States of America.

Many years ago the great British explorer George Mallory, who was to die on Mount Everest, was asked why did he want to climb it. He said, "Because it is there."

Well, space is there, and we're going to climb it, and the moon and the planets are there, and new hopes for knowledge and peace are there. And, therefore, as we set sail we ask God's blessing on the most hazardous and dangerous and greatest adventure on which man has ever embarked.

31 Which statement below best explains the main idea of this passage?

A Space is waiting to be explored.

B Going to the moon is an impossible challenge.

C NASA will play an important role in America's future.

D America will go to the moon and explore space.

32 Which of the following is the author's response to the viewpoint why go into space?

   A Why is the moon so important?

   B Why do people do anything?

   C Why undertake any challenge?

   D Why do mountain climbers exist?

33 Which statement from the passage is a fact that supports the author's argument that going to the moon is a good idea?

   A *There is no strife, no prejudice, no national conflict in outer space as yet.*

   B *. . . five F-1 rocket engines, each one as powerful as all eight engines of the Saturn combined . . .*

   C *This year's space budget is three times what it was in January 1961 . . .*

   D *. . . the space effort . . . has already created a great number of new companies, and tens of thousands of new jobs.*

34 Compare and contrast how the two passages address the importance of the space race. How do the passages describe going into space? Support your answer with quotations and details from both passages. (3 points)

_____

_____

_____

_____

_____

_____

_____

_____

_____

_____

_____

_____

_____

_____

_____

_____

Directions: Read the passage and answer the questions that follow.

NASA Prepares for Return to Moon, Missions Beyond

by Greg Flakus
Houston
17 July 2009
Voice of America News

1   As the world observes the 40th anniversary of the historic moon landing on July 20, 1969, the U.S. agency that accomplished that feat is working on plans for a return to the moon and an even more ambitious plan to use the moon as a base for missions to Mars. The National Aeronautics and Space Administration is gearing up for its biggest challenge yet at a time when funding may be harder to come by.

2   Thousands of people come to the Johnson Space Center in Houston every week to look at some of the rockets and equipment developed back in the 1960s for NASA missions. For many people, those were the glory years, when the Apollo astronauts walked on the moon. But John Connolly, who works with NASA's new lunar project based at the Johnson Space Center, sees even greater things ahead.

3   "There is a new generation of engineers and scientists now at NASA who are eager to get back to the moon to find a lot of those things that Apollo uncovered and that we are finally able to get back to the moon to explore," he said.

4   Engines are firing in tests already under way for the powerful new Ares rockets NASA hopes to use in its Constellation Program, which involves returning to the moon within ten years to establish bases. The missions will count on a much larger lunar landing vehicle and mechanical rovers that can transport both astronauts and equipment around the surface of the orb.

5   John Connolly says there is now evidence that there may be water, in the form of ice, at the moon's poles. In addition, he says study of material brought back from the moon's surface four decades ago shows the availability of oxygen that perhaps can be extracted from the rocks using solar energy.

6   "If you can make all the oxygen that you need at a place like the moon and not have to bring it all the way from earth, you have cut by a factor of 80 percent the mass of stuff you have to bring with you in order to survive in space," he said.

7   But such plans, ambitious as they are, disappoint many space enthusiasts, including the second man to step foot on the moon, in the *Apollo* 11 mission, Edwin *"Buzz"* Aldrin. At a recent appearance here in Houston, he expressed skepticism of the plan that will take another 10 years just to get back to where he was 40 years ago.

8   "Surely there is something not quite right. Maybe we are implementing this wonderful vision in not so smart a way," he said.

9   Others are critical of NASA's plan to abandon the space shuttle next year to

GO ON

concentrate all efforts on the new program. They fear public enthusiasm may wane if years go by without any major missions.

10   Business experts also wonder how a government agency like NASA will fare at a time when the U.S. budget deficit has reached record levels. Chris Bronk, a technology analyst at Rice University, and Troy Gattis, a computer systems architect with Houston's Open Teams software company, recently wrote an editorial suggesting NASA needs to be more like an innovative private company.

11   Chris Bronk says government funding may fall short in the years ahead.

12   "When you look at the manned space mission goals of getting back to the moon, getting to Mars, there is a mandate there that does not equate to the resources that are already provided," he said.

13   The answer, says Gattis, is innovation.

14   "Given the realistic government budgets going forward, if NASA is going to accomplish these great inspirational things, they are going to need this level of innovation that makes space travel become cheaper, easier, faster on a regular basis," he explained.

15   NASA officials say they are aware of the budget restraints. John Connolly says the agency is trying to carry out the mandates from the president and U.S. Congress relying on expertise from within and from experts around the world.

16   "It starts internally at NASA. We have a lot of people who are really smart and who have thought about it for many, many years, like myself. So that is where it starts, but it quickly grows to be a project where we get the input from lots and lots of smart people out there," he said.

17   NASA hopes to do a manned test of the *Orion* launch vehicle by 2015, with the goal of sending a mission to the moon by the year 2020. The *Orion*, which is to be flown into space on the new Ares rocket, includes a launch abort system that will allow the crew module to separate and return to Earth in case of a malfunction. The *Altair* lunar landing craft is being developed to carry up to four astronauts to the moon's surface and allow them to stay there for up to a week.

Directions: Use both "The Decision to Go to the Moon" and "NASA Prepares for Return to the Moon" to answer the following question.

---

35 What is the meaning of the word *lunar* as it is used in paragraph 2?

  A relating to the moon

  B using the moon for travel

  C having the shape of a crescent moon

  D being pale as the Moon compared to the Sun

36 In the first paragraph, the writer claims that NASA may find it difficult to secure funding for its missions. Evaluate the author's reasoning. Does he present any evidence to support this claim? Identify any irrelevant evidence. (5 points)

_____

_____

_____

_____

_____

_____

_____

_____

_____

_____

_____

_____

37 According to the information in paragraphs 1 and 4, how will the Constellation Program be similar to the historic moon landing?

A It will create a base on the moon.

B It will land on the moon.

C It will launch a mission to Mars.

D It will take ten years to accomplish.

38 Which detail from the article best supports the answer to Number 37?

A _As the world observes the 40th anniversary of the historic moon landing on July 20, 1969 . . ._

B _The National Aeronautics and Space Administration is gearing up for its biggest challenge yet . . ._

C _Engines are firing in tests already under way for the powerful new Ares rockets NASA hopes to use in its Constellation Program . . ._

D _. . . the U.S. agency that accomplished that feat is working on plans for a return to the moon . . ._

Take a break. Then go on to Part 3.

Directions: Read the following questions. Then choose the best answer.

---

39 Read the following sentence.

Polly <u>might have been wondering</u> about how to solve the problem.

The underlined words are a—

A participial phrase.

B verb phrase.

C prepositional phrase.

D noun phrase.

40 Read the following sentence.

Patrick decided to cut <u>through the park</u> to save some time.

The underlined words are a—

A participial phrase.

B verb phrase.

C prepositional phrase.

D noun phrase.

41 Which of the following sentences has a relative clause?

A The wolf that usually howled and woke me up at night had disappeared.

B The disappearance of the wolf is a mystery.

C Howling at the moon, the wolf was sitting on a hill.

D The wolf disappeared after howling at the moon.

42 Which of the following sentences has parallel structure?

A Eating chips, to drink pop, and watching TV are a great combination.

B Monique prefers watching movies and eating popcorn.

C To have a relaxing and a time that is wonderful, just go to the cinema.

D Tomas likes to snack on pretzels and eating corn chips while he watches TV.

43 Which sentence contains a participial phrase?

A Afterward, we all laughed at the ridiculousness of it.

B When I went home, I discovered that I had left my bag at school.

C The mayor addressed the crowd's concerns about the transportation crisis.

D Exhausted and stressed out, Darnell closed his textbook.

---

44 Which sentence does NOT include misspelled words?

    A Clarence's behavior last night was abominable.

    B His dessertion from the army was unfortunate.

    C Riley loves to inpersonate people.

    D Everyone idolises our teacher.

45 Which sentence is punctuated correctly?

    A "I need to make a list, Mrs. Johnson muttered."

    B I have so many things to do: cook supper, send emails, and babysit the kids.

    C Supper is usually something simple spaghetti is a common choice.

    D After I finish the laundry; I will help with homework.

46 Which sentence is NOT punctuated correctly?

    A The Millers planted a young tree in their yard; a young tree is called a sapling.

    B Trees come in many types: oak, ash, birch, aspen, cedar, and more.

    C Mr. Miller suggested, "Let's put another sapling over here."

    D Mr. and Mrs. Miller bought another tree, they planted it near the first one.

47 Which sentence uses correct capitalization?

    A She wrote an essay called "My Favorite Movies."

    B Becca loves three movies: Frozen, the Princess Bride, and Wild Hearts Can't Be Broken.

    C Becca's dad, Dr. baird, liked her essay.

    D Becca wants to someday work for a company such as Universal studios.

48 Which sentence uses correct capitalization?

    A Mark Twain wrote a story called "the Celebrated Jumping Frog of Calaveras County."

    B It was published in The Saturday press in November of 1865.

    C It was later republished as part of a book by the publishing company, Harper and Brothers.

    D Mark Twain's real name is Samuel langhorne Clemens, and he was born in Missouri in 1835.

49 Which sentence does NOT include misspelled words?

    A Joaquin accidentally delleted the paper from his computer.

    B I know it was not deliberate.

    C Now, as a prekaution, we save our work on a flash drive, too.

    D We will not have a disastrus push of a button again.

50 Rewrite the following sentence so that it has parallel structure. (1 point)

Sai visited her family in Seattle and saw the Space Needle, hiked up Mount Rainier, and going to Pike's Place Fish Market.

_____

_____

_____

_____

Points Earned/Total = _____/70

Reading Literature Lesson 1

Cite, Infer, and Summarize

Review the Standards (RL.9.1, RL.9.2, W.9.9a)

- Cite textual evidence to support analysis of a text
- Draw inferences from a text
- Summarize a text

Q: What is **textual evidence?**

A: Direct quotations from the text that support a point or answer a question are **textual evidence**. When answering questions or writing about a text, you will often be asked to cite, or give, evidence to support your answer.

Q: What is an **inference**?

A: An **inference** is a reasonable guess. To draw an inference, you combine clues from the text and information you already know. For example, if a character goes for a jog every morning, you can infer that the character is in good shape.

Q: How do I **summarize** a story?

A: A **summary** of a story should include the setting, the main characters, and the major events explained in chronological order. Do not include minor characters, minor events, or your opinions.

 Try It

Directions: Read the passage. Then answer the questions that follow.

O Pioneers!

by Willa Cather

To-night, after they sat down to supper, Oscar kept looking at Lou as if he expected him to say something, and Lou blinked his eyes and frowned at his plate. It was Alexandra herself who at last opened the discussion.

"The Linstrums," she said calmly, as she put another plate of hot biscuits on the table, "are going back to St. Louis. The old man is going to work in the cigar factory again."

At this Lou plunged in. "You see, Alexandra, everybody who can crawl out is going away. There's no use of us trying to stick it out, just to be stubborn. There's something in knowing when to quit."

"Where do you want to go, Lou?"

"Any place where things will grow," said Oscar grimly.

GO ON

Lou reached for a potato. "Chris Arnson has traded his half-section for a place down on the river."

"Who did he trade with?"

"Charley Fuller, in town."

"Fuller the real estate man? You see, Lou, that Fuller has a head on him. He's buying and trading for every bit of land he can get up here. It'll make him a rich man, some day."

"He's rich now, that's why he can take a chance."

"Why can't we? We'll live longer than he will. Some day the land itself will be worth more than all we can ever raise on it."

Lou laughed. "It could be worth that, and still not be worth much. Why, Alexandra, you don't know what you're talking about. Our place wouldn't bring now what it would six years ago. The fellows that settled up here just made a mistake. Now they're beginning to see this high land wasn't never meant to grow nothing on, and everybody who ain't fixed to graze cattle is trying to crawl out. It's too high to farm up here. All the Americans are skinning out. That man Percy Adams, north of town, told me that he was going to let Fuller take his land and stuff for four hundred dollars and a ticket to Chicago."

"There's Fuller again!" Alexandra exclaimed. "I wish that man would take me for a partner. He's feathering his nest! If only poor people could learn a little from rich people! But all these fellows who are running off are bad farmers, like poor Mr. Linstrum. They couldn't get ahead even in good years, and they all got into debt while father was getting out. I think we ought to hold on as long as we can on father's account. He was so set on keeping this land. He must have seen harder times than this, here. How was it in the early days, mother?"

1 All of the following could be used as evidence to support the idea that Oscar and Lou want to sell the family farm EXCEPT?

   A Alexandra told Oscar and Lou that the Linstrums were going back to St. Louis.

   B Lou says, "everybody who can crawl out is going away."

   C Oscar tells Alexandra that he wants to go any place where things will grow.

   D Lou says, "it's too high to farm up here."

2 We can infer that Alexandra's attitude is calm because—

   A she wants to sell the farm too.

   B she knows the farm is worthless.

   C she realizes she cannot stop Oscar and Lou from selling the farm.

   D she already knew that Lou and Oscar wanted to sell the farm.

3 Write a summary of the story. Be sure to include the setting, characters, and main events. (3 points)

   _____

   _____

   _____

   _____

_____

_____

_____

_____

_____

_____

4 Why does Alexandra bring her father into the discussion? How does this action affect her argument for keeping the farm?

_____

_____

_____

_____

_____

_____

_____

_____

_____

_____

For **Example 1**, you must evaluate which **evidence** from the text supports the idea that Oscar and Lou want to sell the farm. Evidence from the story that shows they want to sell includes what Lou says about people leaving the area and the altitude making farming difficult (choices B and D) and what Oscar says about going any place where things can grow (choice D). Choice A does not support the idea, so **choice A** is the correct answer.

Example 2 asks you to make an **inference** about why Alexandra has a calm attitude. Alexandra argues against selling the farm, so choice A is incorrect. Eliminate choices B and C because the going price of the farm and who holds the final say in selling the farm is never referred to in the story. Because Alexandra herself initiates the discussion and she does not indicate any surprise that Lou and Oscar argue for selling the farm, we can infer that Alexandra was already aware that they wanted to sell. **Choice D** is correct.

For **Example 3**, you must write a **summary** of the story. Remember that a good summary includes the setting, main characters, and main events.

Good: *During supper, Oscar, Lou, and Alexandra debate about selling the family farm. Lou claims that many people are leaving because they have realized the land is not farmable. Alexandra argues that only the bad farmers are leaving and that their father*

GO ON →

would not want them to sell the land.

This is a poor response because it leaves out key details from the passage.

Poor: *Lou and Oscar talk to Alexandra about selling the family farm. Lou and Oscar want to leave, but Alexandra wants to stay.*

For **Example 4**, you must cite **evidence** from the story to support your analysis. A good answer will rephrase the question, draw a conclusion, and include specific evidence to support that conclusion.

Good: *Alexandra mentions her father's wishes to support her opinion. Alexandra uses her father as an example of a good farmer who was able to get out of debt to counter Lou's claims that all of the area farmers are realizing they simply can't farm the land. She also points out that her father was determined to hold on to the land, which further strengthens her position.*

 Try It On Your Own

Directions: Read the passage. Then answer the questions that follow.

The Family Farm

After the buyer's agent left, the family sat around the suddenly silent table. Their eyes determinedly avoided each other, staring fixedly at the worn but polished wood on the table or leaping randomly around the room, glancing at the clock on the mantel, the smoldering logs in the fireplace, or the ominous pile of papers piled at one end of the table. No one dared to break the oppressive silence that permeated the old farmhouse. Finally, Jessamie rose abruptly and the sound of her chair scraping against the wood floor jolted Ben and Lila out of their reverie. Their eyes met and quickly skittered away.

"Let's get supper started," Jessamie announced to the room.

The family gratefully fell into a familiar routine. Lila and Ben set the table for three while Jessamie filled serving dishes with food and deposited each on a hot pad in the center of the table. As Ben filled each glass with water from the pitcher, Jessamie nodded at Lila, who began scooping food onto her plate.

After the meal, the three siblings cleared the dishes and retired to the well worn chairs in front of the fireplace. Jessamie added a log to the dying embers and turned to Lila and Ben.

"So what do you think about selling the farm to Mr. Baker?" Jessamie was proud that she asked the question in an even tone of voice.

A moment of crystalline silence greeted her question. Lila watched her hands twist nervously in her lap, while Ben stared doggedly at his feet, planted in front of his chair.

Lila took a quick breath and said, "I think it's a good idea to sell. The farm is too much for us to work on our own, and I never really wanted to be a farmer anyway." Her words ran together as she spoke, as though she forced them all out in one breath.

Jessamie nodded slowly, and then looked at Ben, asking, "What do you think, Ben? Do you want to sell?"

"I don't know," Ben muttered.

"I know it's hard to think about selling the farm. Mom and Dad worked so hard to buy this land and wanted us to take it over. But they are both gone now, so we have to think about what we want to do with the rest of our lives," Jessamie stated.

Lila's face was white and set as she explained, "It feels like we're letting them down or giving up, but this farm was their dream, not mine."

"What do you think?" Ben asked Jessamie.

Jessamie paused, "It's a hard thing to decide since we've all grown up here, but I lean toward selling and taking our chances that way. Aunt Mary has been after us to live with her and help with her bakery. And then, Ben, you and Lila could go to college, and you could study to be a vet if you still wanted to."

Jessamie rose and gazed out the window at the twilight glazing the countryside in shadows. "It seems to me that if we stay, we might be able to work the farm together or we might lose it, but if we leave, we have the chance to do other things. So I say we sell."

At these words, Ben and Lila rose also and stood beside Jessamie at the window. All three stood a little straighter as if a great weight had been lifted from their shoulders. The gloom and uncertainty that hovered over the atmosphere dissipated as frost beneath the morning sun. As the shadows darkened and blanketed the outdoors, the light blazed even more brightly inside the house.

5 How does Lila influence the action of the story? Cite evidence from the text to support your answer. (3 points)

_____

_____

_____

_____

_____

_____

_____

_____

_____

_____

_____

_____

_____

_____

GO ON

6 Based upon the passage, we can infer that—

    A Lila wants to become a doctor.

    B Ben doesn't care about the farm.

    C Aunt Mary is a hard worker.

    D Jessamie is the oldest sibling.

7 Which of the following details should be included in a good summary of the story?

    A Ben and Lila set the table for supper.

    B Lila's words ran all together as she spoke.

    C Jessamie suggests they sell the farm.

    D Ben rose and stood next to Jessamie.

Character and Theme

Review the Standards (RL.9.2, RL.9.3, RL.9.9)

- Explain how a **theme** is developed and how it is shaped by specific details
- Analyze how **complex characters** develop and interact to advance the plot or develop the theme
- Analyze how a modern work of fiction draws on themes, patterns of events, or character types from myths, traditional stories, or religious works

Q: How does a **theme** develop?

A: A **theme** is a main idea or lesson. The characters, setting, and plot build the theme. When reading literature, analyze how an author describes the characters and setting. A detailed description of a character or place may point toward a theme, and specific details that are repeated or emphasized can also be thematic. Ask, "What does the character learn from this conflict" and "Do these details seem designed to draw my attention to an idea or truth?"

Q: How do **complex characters** develop and interact?

A: Complex characters often change over the course of a story. In the beginning of a story, a character may hold a certain belief or act in one way, but a conflict forces her to discover a hidden strength, learn something new, or decide how to face a challenge. In addition, how characters interact with one another often changes as well since plot events also influence the relationships between or among characters. These changes move the story forward.

Q: What are some ways that modern literature draws on works from the past?

A: Modern works of literature sometimes use traditional ideas, plots, or character types in new or surprising ways. For example, modern literature often uses the "hero" character found in ancient myths and stories. However, modern heroes may fight against prejudice instead of one-eyed monsters.

 Try It

Directions: Read the passage. Then answer the questions that follow.

The Open Window

by Saki

"You may wonder why we keep that window wide open on an October afternoon," said the niece, indicating a large French window that opened on to a lawn.

"It is quite warm for the time of the year," said Framton; "but has that window got anything to do with the tragedy?"

GO ON ➡

"Out through that window, three years ago to a day, her husband and her two young brothers went off for their day's shooting. They never came back. In crossing the moor to their favourite snipe-shooting ground they were all three engulfed in a treacherous piece of bog. It had been that dreadful wet summer, you know, and places that were safe in other years gave way suddenly without warning. Their bodies were never recovered. That was the dreadful part of it." Here the child's voice lost its self-possessed note and became falteringly human. "Poor aunt always thinks that they will come back some day, they and the little brown spaniel that was lost with them, and walk in at that window just as they used to do. That is why the window is kept open every evening till it is quite dusk. Poor dear aunt, she has often told me how they went out, her husband with his white waterproof coat over his arm, and Ronnie, her youngest brother, singing 'Bertie, why do you bound?' as he always did to tease her, because she said it got on her nerves. Do you know, sometimes on still, quiet evenings like this, I almost get a creepy feeling that they will all walk in through that window—"

She broke off with a little shudder. It was a relief to Framton when the aunt bustled into the room with a whirl of apologies for being late in making her appearance.

"I hope Vera has been amusing you?" she said.

"She has been very interesting," said Framton.

"I hope you don't mind the open window," said Mrs. Sappleton briskly; "my husband and brothers will be home directly from shooting, and they always come in this way. They've been out for snipe in the marshes to-day, so they'll make a fine mess over my poor carpets. So like you men-folk, isn't it?"

She rattled on cheerfully about the shooting and the scarcity of birds, and the prospects for duck in the winter. To Framton it was all purely horrible. He made a desperate but only partially successful effort to turn the talk on to a less ghastly topic; he was conscious that his hostess was giving him only a fragment of her attention, and her eyes were constantly straying past him to the open window and the lawn beyond. It was certainly an unfortunate coincidence that he should have paid his visit on this tragic anniversary.

"The doctors agree in ordering me complete rest, an absence of mental excitement, and avoidance of anything in the nature of violent physical exercise," announced Framton, who laboured under the tolerably widespread delusion that total strangers and chance acquaintances are hungry for the least detail of one's ailments and infirmities, their cause and cure. "On the matter of diet they are not so much in agreement," he continued.

"No?" said Mrs. Sappleton, in a voice which only replaced a yawn at the last moment. Then she suddenly brightened into alert attention—but not to what Framton was saying.

"Here they are at last!" she cried. "Just in time for tea, and don't they look as if they were muddy up to the eyes!"

Framton shivered slightly and turned towards the niece with a look intended to convey sympathetic comprehension. The child was staring out through the open window with dazed horror in her eyes. In a chill shock of nameless fear Framton swung round in his seat and looked in the same direction.

In the deepening twilight three figures were walking across the lawn towards the window; they all carried guns under their arms, and one of them was additionally burdened with a white coat hung over his shoulders. A tired brown spaniel kept close at their heels. Noiselessly they neared the house, and then a hoarse young voice chanted out of the dusk: "I said, Bertie, why do you bound?"

Framton grabbed wildly at his stick and hat; the hall-door, the gravel-drive, and the front gate were dimly-noted stages in his headlong retreat. A cyclist coming along the road had to run into the hedge to avoid an imminent collision.

"Here we are, my dear," said the bearer of the white mackintosh, coming in through the window; "fairly muddy, but most of it's dry. Who was that who bolted out as we came up?"

"A most extraordinary man, a Mr. Nuttel," said Mrs. Sappleton; "could only talk about his illnesses, and dashed off without a word of good-bye or apology when you arrived. One would think he had seen a ghost."

"I expect it was the spaniel," said the niece calmly; "he told me he had a horror of dogs. He was once hunted into a cemetery somewhere on the banks of the Ganges by a pack of pariah dogs, and had to spend the night in a newly dug grave with the creatures snarling and grinning and foaming just above him. Enough to make anyone lose their nerve."

Romance at short notice was her speciality.

---

1   What is the theme of this story?

   A A creative imagination can lead to mischief.

   B Loyalty is the most important quality to possess.

   C Life is full of the unexpected.

   D A person's fears must be overcome.

2   Which traditional character is Vera most like?

   A Snow White, who hid from her evil stepmother

   B Hansel, who lost his way in the forest

   C Sleeping Beauty, who fell under an evil spell

   D Loki, who is the Norse trickster god

3   Write a summary of the story. Be sure to include the setting, characters, and main events.

   _____

   _____

   _____

   _____

   _____

   _____

   _____

   _____

   _____

   _____

4 How does Vera's storytelling ability contribute to Framton's fleeing the house? (3 points)

_____

_____

_____

_____

_____

_____

_____

_____

_____

For **Example 1**, you must identify the theme of the story. To identify a theme, you need to think about characters, setting, and plot.

Characters: Vera likes to make up stories, and Framton is a gullible person.

Setting: The story takes place in a house, where Framton believes a tragedy has occurred.

Plot: Vera relates a tale that causes Framton to question the sanity of the mistress of the house and then to flee in terror when he sees figures approaching the house through the open window.

You can determine that the best answer is **choice A**.

Example 2 asks you to compare Vera, a character in a modern story, to characters in traditional stories to determine which character she is most like. Vera does not get lost in the forest, fall under a spell, or hide from an evil relative, so you can eliminate choices A, B, and C. She does play tricks on people, much like a trickster god would do. **Choice D** is correct.

For **Example 3**, you must summarize the story.

Good: _Vera relates to a guest named Framton a fabricated story of how her aunt lost her husband and two brothers on a hunting trip and adds that her aunt is under the impression that they will return today on the anniversary of the "tragedy." Framton believes Vera's tale and is shocked and frightened when he actually sees three figures moving toward the house. He bolts away, and Vera's aunt is perplexed by his strange behavior until Vera spins another tall tale about Framton having a fear of dogs._

This is a poor response because it leaves out key details from the passage.

Poor: _Framton runs from the house after he sees three people coming toward the house because Vera has caused him to believe that they are the ghosts of his host's husband and brothers._

For **Example 4**, you must think about how Vera's storytelling helps move the plot forward. A good response includes specific details from the passage to support your answer.

© **Perfection Learning®** **No reproduction permitted.**

Good: *Vera's gifted storytelling makes her tale all the more believable to Framton, which causes him to run from the house. Vera uses details such as "a little brown spaniel" and the singing of "Bertie, why do you bound?" to lend credibility to her story. As a consequence, Framton wholeheartedly believes he is seeing ghosts and rushes away when he sees the figures returning to the house. Vera's dialogue with Framton is the backbone of the story.*

This is a poor response because it leaves out key details from the passage.

Poor: *Vera tells the story about the tragedy so well that it makes Framton believe her, so he rushes away when the hunting group returns.*

Try It On Your Own

Directions: Read the passage. Then answer the questions that follow.

Dead Men's Path

by Chinua Achebe

[. . .] Three days later the village priest of Ani called on the headmaster. He was an old man and walked with a slight stoop. He carried a stout walking stick which he usually tapped on the floor, by way of emphasis, each time he made a new point in his argument.

"I have heard," he said after the usual exchange of cordialities, "that our ancestral footpath has recently been closed . . ."

"Yes," replied Mr. Obi. "We cannot allow people to make a highway of our school compound."

"Look here, my son," said the priest bringing down his walking-stick, "this path was here before you were born and before your father was born. The whole life of this village depends on it. Our dead relatives depart by it and our ancestors visit us by it. But most important, it is the path of children coming in to be born . . ."

Mr. Obi listened with a satisfied smile on his face.

"The whole purpose of our school," he said finally, "is to eradicate just such beliefs as that. Dead men do not require footpaths. The whole idea is just fantastic. Our duty is to teach your children to laugh at such ideas."

"What you say may be true," replied the priest, "but we follow the practices of our fathers. If you re-open the path we shall have nothing to quarrel about. What I always say is: let the hawk perch and let the eagle perch."

He rose to go.

"I am sorry," said the young headmaster. "But the school compound cannot be a thoroughfare. It is against our regulations. I would suggest your constructing another path, skirting our premises. We can even get our boys to help in building it. I don't suppose the ancestors will find the little detour too burdensome."

"I have no more words to say," said the old priest, already outside.

Two days later a young woman in the village died in childbed. A diviner was immediately consulted and he prescribed heavy sacrifices to propitiate ancestors insulted by the fence.

Obi woke up the next morning among the ruins of his work. The beautiful hedges were torn up not just near the path but right round the school, the flowers trampled to death and one of the school buildings pulled down . . .

That day, the white Supervisor came to inspect the school and wrote a nasty report on the state of the premises but more seriously about the "tribal-war situation developing between the school and the village, arising in part from the misguided zeal of the new headmaster."

---

5 What is Mr. Obi's greatest fault in the story? Describe how his actions and words show this flaw. Use at least two details from the passage to support your answer. (3 points)

_____

_____

_____

_____

_____

_____

_____

_____

_____

_____

_____

_____

6 What is the theme of this story?

A Modern ways are the best ways.

B Ghosts are real.

C Talk is cheap.

D Elders deserve respect.

7 How does the author use action to show that the villagers are angry about the footpath closure?

   A by having the priest come and talk to Mr. Obi

   B by having the priest bang his walking-stick

   C by having Obi see the destruction around the school

   D by having the superintendent write a negative report

8 The priest meets with Mr. Obi to convince him to reopen the path. He is MOST like—

   A a lion who befriends a mouse and subsequently declares, "Tiny friends can be great friends."

   B a man in a Native American tale who tries to convince white people to stop slaughtering the buffalo.

   C a king who holds a contest for the strongest and best knight to win his daughter's hand in marriage.

   D a boy who finds a magic lamp and is granted three wishes by the lamp's genie.

Test-Taking Tips

1 To cite evidence to support your answer, go back to the story and look for details, dialogue, or events that help make your answer clear or correct.

2 To draw inferences, look for details in the passage to support your answer. Combine the clues with your own knowledge and experience to figure out the correct answer.

3 Questions about a work's theme are asking you about the work's main idea or lesson. Think about the problem or conflict in the story and how the main character solves it. Think about what the main character learns from the conflict.

4 To analyze how a modern work uses themes, patterns of events, or character types found in traditional literature, ask yourself questions such as the following: *Do these stories teach a similar lesson? Do these characters face a similar problem or challenge? What personality traits do these characters share?*

Go for it!

Unit One Practice Test

Directions: Read the passage. Then answer the questions that follow.

The Story of an Hour

by Kate Chopin

1   Knowing that Mrs. Mallard was afflicted with heart trouble, great care was taken to break to her as gently as possible the news of her husband's death.

2   It was her sister Josephine who told her, in broken sentences; veiled hints that revealed in half concealing. Her husband's friend Richards was there, too, near her. It was he who had been in the newspaper office when intelligence of the railroad disaster was received, with Brently Mallard's name leading the list of "killed." He had only taken the time to assure himself of its truth by a second telegram, and had hastened to forestall any less careful, less tender friend in bearing the sad message.

3   She did not hear the story as many women have heard the same, with a paralyzed inability to accept its significance. She wept at once, with sudden, wild abandonment, in her sister' s arms. When the storm of grief had spent itself she went away to her room alone. She would have no one follow her.

4   There stood, facing the open window, a comfortable, roomy armchair. Into this she sank, pressed down by a physical exhaustion that haunted her body and seemed to reach into her soul.

5   She could see in the open square before her house the tops of trees that were all aquiver with the new spring life. The delicious breath of rain was in the air. In the street below a peddler was crying his wares. The notes of a distant song which someone was singing reached her faintly, and countless sparrows were twittering in the eaves.

6   There were patches of blue sky showing here and there through the clouds that had met and piled one above the other in the west facing her window.

7   She sat with her head thrown back upon the cushion of the chair, quite motionless, except when a sob came up into her throat and shook her, as a child who has cried itself to sleep continues to sob in its dreams.

8   She was young, with a fair, calm face, whose lines bespoke repression and even a certain strength. But now there was a dull stare in her eyes, whose gaze was fixed away off yonder on one of those patches of blue sky. It was not a glance of reflection, but rather indicated a suspension of intelligent thought.

9   There was something coming to her and she was waiting for it, fearfully. What was it? She did not know; it was too subtle and elusive to name. But she felt it, creeping out of the sky, reaching toward her through the sounds, the scents, the color that filled the air.

10   Now her bosom rose and fell tumultuously. She was beginning to recognize this thing that was approaching to possess her, and she was striving to beat it back with her will—as powerless as her two white slender hands would have been. When she abandoned herself a little whispered word escaped her slightly parted lips. She said it over and over under her breath: "free, free, free!" The

vacant stare and the look of terror that had followed it went from her eyes. They stayed keen and bright. Her pulses beat fast, and the coursing blood warmed and relaxed every inch of her body.

11   She did not stop to ask if it were or were not a monstrous joy that held her. A clear and exalted perception enabled her to dismiss the suggestion as trivial. She knew that she would weep again when she saw the kind, tender hands folded in death; the face that had never looked save with love upon her, fixed and gray and dead. But she saw beyond that bitter moment a long procession of years to come that would belong to her absolutely. And she opened and spread her arms out to them in welcome.

12   There would be no one to live for during those coming years; she would live for herself. There would be no powerful will bending hers in that blind persistence with which men and women believe they have a right to impose a private will upon a fellow-creature. A kind intention or a cruel intention made the act seem no less a crime as she looked upon it in that brief moment of illumination.

13   And yet she had loved him—sometimes. Often she had not. What did it matter! What could love, the unsolved mystery, count for in the face of this possession of self-assertion which she suddenly recognized as the strongest impulse of her being!

14   "Free! Body and soul free!" she kept whispering.

15   Josephine was kneeling before the closed door with her lips to the keyhole, imploring for admission. "Louise, open the door! I beg; open the door—you will make yourself ill. What are you doing, Louise? For heaven's sake open the door."

16   "Go away. I am not making myself ill." No; she was drinking in a very elixir of life through that open window.

17   Her fancy was running riot along those days ahead of her. Spring days, and summer days, and all sorts of days that would be her own. She breathed a quick prayer that life might be long. It was only yesterday she had thought with a shudder that life might be long.

18   She arose at length and opened the door to her sister's importunities. There was a feverish triumph in her eyes, and she carried herself unwittingly like a goddess of Victory. She clasped her sister's waist, and together they descended the stairs. Richards stood waiting for them at the bottom.

19   Someone was opening the front door with a latchkey. It was Brently Mallard who entered, a little travel-stained, composedly carrying his grip-sack and umbrella. He had been far from the scene of the accident, and did not even know there had been one. He stood amazed at Josephine's piercing cry; at Richards' quick motion to screen him from the view of his wife.

20   When the doctors came they said she had died of heart disease—of the joy that kills.

---

1 Which sentence from the story shows that people believe that Louise is fragile?

   A *Knowing that Mrs. Mallard was afflicted with heart trouble, great care was taken to break to her as gently as possible the news of her husband's death.*

   B *He had only taken the time to assure himself of its truth by a second telegram.*

   C *Into this she sank, pressed down by a physical exhaustion that haunted her body and seemed to reach into her soul.*

   D *She clasped her sister's waist, and together they descended the stairs.*

GO ON

2 On the lines below, write a summary of "The Story of an Hour." Include the setting, the main characters, and the main events. (3 points)

_____

_____

_____

_____

_____

_____

_____

_____

_____

_____

_____

_____

_____

3 Louise in this story can be compared to which character type from traditional literature?

   A a wicked witch

   B a deceitful coyote

   C a damsel in distress

   D a genie in a lamp

4 Based on Louise's actions in the story, you can infer that she—

   A hates her husband.

   B is a bad wife.

   C lies about her heart disease.

   D feels trapped in her marriage.

5 Which detail from the passage supports the idea that Richards is a caring person?

   A Richards is Brently Mallard's friend.

   B Richards first hears of Brently's death.

   C Richards wants to tell Louise the news gently.

   D Richards waits at the bottom of the stairs.

6 Which best expresses the theme of the selection?

    A The unexpected adds zest to life.

    B People should be free to make their own choices.

    C Family is more important than anything else.

    D Be careful what you wish for.

7 What does Louise's dialogue and thoughts in paragraphs 10 and 11 reveal about her character? (3 points)

_____

_____

_____

_____

_____

_____

_____

_____

_____

_____

_____

_____

_____

8 What causes Louise to leave her room?

    A She learns that her husband is actually alive.

    B She needs support from her sister in her time of grief.

    C She is ready to seize new opportunities open to her.

    D She wants to reassure everyone that she is all right.

STOP

Points Earned/Total = _____ /12

Reading Literature Lesson 3

Word Choice

Review the Standards (RL.9.4, L.9.5a, L.9.5.b)

- Interpret **figurative language**
- Analyze the impact of **word choice** on meaning and **tone**
- Determine **connotation** and **nuances** in meanings of words with similar denotations

Q: What is **figurative language**?

A: Figurative language suggests something other than the literal meaning of the words. Examples of figurative language are similes, metaphors, and personification. To answer questions about figurative language, think about what ideas or emotions the author is trying to convey.

Q: How does an author's **word choice** affect meaning and **tone**?

A: Writers choose their words carefully to communicate **tone**, or the writer's attitude or feeling toward the subject matter. You can also judge the tone of the writing based upon the analogies, or comparisons and allusions, or references to other works, the writer uses. For example, if the writer compares his main character to a lost little lamb, the tone is sympathetic. You can usually describe a work's tone using adjectives, such as formal, sarcastic, pessimistic, longing, or sad.

Q: What is **connotation** and how does **nuance** affect words with similar denotations?

A: A word's **connotation** is the feeling suggested beyond the word's meaning. For example, although house and home are synonyms, a home implies a family and more of a personal attachment, whereas a house is a more impersonal type of residence. Nuance is the slight difference between two words that have very similar dictionary meanings. **Nuance** are shades of meaning. For example, saying the summer heat is scorching suggests it is extremely hot outside, while saying it is sweltering implies that it is extremely hot as well as humid.

➲ Try It

Directions: Read the passage. Then answer the questions that follow.

from Out of Africa

by Isak Dinesen

    I had a farm in Africa, at the foot of the Ngong Hills. The Equator runs across these highlands, a hundred miles to the North, and the farm lay at an altitude of over six thousand feet. In the daytime you felt that you had got high up, near to the sun, but the early mornings and evenings were limpid and restful, and the nights were cold. The geographical position, and the height of the land combined to create a landscape that had not its like in all the world. There was no fat on it and no luxuriance anywhere; it was Africa distilled up through six thousand feet, like the strong and refined essence of a continent. The colors were dry and burnt, like the colors in pottery. The trees had a light delicate foliage, the structure of which was different from that of the trees in Europe; it did not grow in bows or cupolas, but in horizontal layers, and the formation gave to the tall solitary trees a likeness to the palms, or a heroic and romantic air like fullrigged ships with their sails clewed up, and to the edge of a wood a strange appearance as if the whole wood were faintly vibrating. Upon the grass of the great plains the crooked bare old thorntrees were scattered, and the grass was spiced like thyme and bog-myrtle; in some places the scent was so strong, that it smarted in the nostrils. All the flowers that you found on the plains, or upon the creepers and liana in the native forest, were diminutive like flowers of the downs,—only just in the beginning of the long rains a number of big, massive heavy-scented lilies sprang out on the plains. The views were immensely wide. Everything that you saw made for greatness and freedom, and unequalled nobility.

The chief feature of the landscape, and of your life in it, was the air. Looking back on a sojourn in the African highlands, you are struck by your feeling of having lived for a time up in the air. The sky was rarely more than pale blue or violet, with a profusion of mighty, weightless, ever-changing clouds towering up and sailing on it, but it has a blue vigor in it, and at a short distance it painted the ranges of hills and the woods a fresh deep blue. In the middle of the day the air was alive over the land, like a flame burning; it scintillated, waved and shone like running water, mirrored and doubled all objects, and created great Fata Morgana (a mirage). Up in this high air you breathed easily, drawing in a vital assurance and lightness of heart. In the highlands you woke up in the morning and thought: Here I am, where I ought to be.

---

1   Which word or phrase from the passage is used to communicate a feeling of sudden development?

   A *grow*

   B *scattered*

   C *sprang out*

   D *created*

2   Air that is <u>alive over the land, like a flame burning</u> probably—

   A catches fire.

   B slows down.

   C disappears.

   D shimmers.

3   Which word from the passage is used to communicate a feeling of vastness?

   A *strong*

   B *immensely*

   C *chief*

   D *vital*

4 What is the tone of the story? Give examples of how the author's word choice sets the tone of the story. (3 points)

_____

_____

_____

_____

_____

_____

_____

_____

_____

_____

To answer **Example 1,** think about the **connotations** of each answer choice. While each choice expresses an action, only *sprang out* has connotations of sudden growth or development. **Choice C** is correct. The other choices express fairly neutral connotations of development or distribution.

A **simile** is figurative language that describes something by comparing two things that are not alike. Similes use the words *like* and *as* to compare two things. **Example 2** is a simile that says the air was like a flame burning. To answer this question, you need to think about how a burning flame looks and then how the air could look like that. The answer is **choice D**, *shimmers*.

To answer **Example 3,** think about the connotations of each answer choice. All are adjectives, but only *immensely* has connotations of hugeness and enormity. **Choice B** is correct. The other choices express connotations of strength or importance.

For **Example 4,** you must identify and explain the tone of the story. A good response includes specific examples from the passage to support your answer.

Good: *The tone of the story is dreamlike, showing the writer's nostalgic reminiscenses about living on the farm in Africa. Descriptive sentences use surreal figures of speech, such as the air "waved and shone like running water" and the edge of the forest was "faintly vibrating." Descriptions such as "a heroic and romantic air," "mighty, weightless, ever-changing clouds," and "having lived for a time up in the air" contribute to the dreamlike tone. The tone reveals a dreamlike nostalgia toward the African farm.*

This is a poor response because it doesn't use examples from the story.

Poor: *The tone is the writer's feeling toward what he or she is writing about. You can look at words in the story to figure out the tone. This can be a challenge, like in the story about living on an African farm.*

Directions: Read the passage. Then answer the questions that follow.

from **The Happy Prince**

by Oscar Wilde

"It is winter," answered the Swallow, "and the chill snow will soon be here. In Egypt the sun is warm on the green palm-trees, and the crocodiles lie in the mud and look lazily about them. My companions are building a nest in the Temple of Baalbec, and the pink and white doves are watching them, and cooing to each other. Dear Prince, I must leave you, but I will never forget you, and next spring I will bring you back two beautiful jewels in place of those you have given away. The ruby shall be redder than a red rose, and the sapphire shall be <u>as blue as the great sea</u>."

"In the square below," said the Happy Prince, "there stands a little match-girl. She has let her matches fall in the gutter, and they are all spoiled. Her father will beat her if she does not bring home some money, and she is crying. She has no shoes or stockings, and her little head is bare. Pluck out my other eye and give it to her, and her father will not beat her."

"I will stay with you one night longer," said the Swallow, "but I cannot pluck out your eye. You would be quite blind then."

"Swallow, Swallow, little Swallow," said the Prince, "do as I command you."

So he plucked out the Prince's other eye, and darted down with it. He swooped past the match-girl, and slipped the jewel into the palm of her hand. "What a lovely bit of glass!" cried the little girl; and she ran home, laughing.

Then the Swallow came back to the Prince. "You are blind now," he said, "so I will stay with you always."

"No, little Swallow," said the poor Prince, "you must go away to Egypt."

"I will stay with you always," said the Swallow, and he slept at the Prince's feet.

All the next day he sat on the Prince's shoulder, and told him stories of what he had seen in strange lands. He told him of the red ibises, who stand in long rows on the banks of the Nile, and catch gold-fish in their beaks; of the Sphinx, <u>who is as old as the world itself</u>, and lives in the desert, and knows everything; of the merchants, who walk slowly by the side of their camels and carry amber beads in their hands; of the King of the Mountains of the Moon, who is as black as ebony, and worships a large crystal; of the great green snake that sleeps in a palm tree, and has twenty priests to feed it with honey-cakes; and of the pygmies who sail over a big lake on large flat leaves, and are always at war with the butterflies.

"Dear little Swallow," said the Prince, "you tell me of marvellous things, but more marvellous than anything is the suffering of men and of women. There is no Mystery so great as Misery. Fly over my city, little Swallow, and tell me what you see there."

So the Swallow flew over the great city, and saw the rich making merry in their beautiful houses, while the beggars were sitting at the gates. He flew into dark lanes, and saw the white faces of starving children looking out listlessly at the black streets. Under the archway of a bridge two little boys were lying in one another's arms to try and keep themselves warm. "How hungry we are!" they said. "You must not lie here," shouted the Watchman, and they wandered out into the rain.

Then he flew back and told the Prince what he had seen.

"I am covered with fine gold," said the Prince, "you must take it off, leaf by leaf, and give it to my poor; the living always think that gold can make them happy."

Leaf after leaf of the fine gold the Swallow picked off, till the Happy Prince looked quite dull and grey. Leaf after leaf of the fine gold he brought to the poor, and the children's faces grew rosier, and they laughed and played games in the street. "We have bread now!" they cried.

Then the snow came, and after the snow came the frost. The streets looked as if they were made of silver, they were so bright and glistening; long icicles like crystal daggers hung down from the eaves of the houses, everybody went about in furs, and the little boys wore scarlet caps and skated on the ice.

The poor little Swallow grew colder and colder, but he would not leave the Prince, he loved him too well. He picked up crumbs outside the baker's door when the baker was not looking, and tried to keep himself warm by flapping his wings.

But at last he knew that he was going to die. He had just strength to fly up to the Prince's shoulder once more. "Good-bye, dear Prince!" he murmured, "will you let me kiss your hand?"

"I am glad that you are going to Egypt at last, little Swallow," said the Prince, "you have stayed too long here; but you must kiss me on the lips, for I love you."

"It is not to Egypt that I am going," said the Swallow. "I am going to the House of Death. Death is the brother of Sleep, is he not?"

And he kissed the Happy Prince on the lips, and fell down dead at his feet.

At that moment a curious crack sounded inside the statue, as if something had broken. The fact is that the leaden heart had snapped right in two. It certainly was a dreadfully hard frost.

---

5 The children are described as "looking out listlessly at the black streets? They are probably listless because

A they are bored.

B they are cold.

C they aren't allowed to go out.

D they are hungry.

6 What does the simile, the sapphire was "as blue as the great sea" mean?

A The sapphire's color resembled the blue of the sea.

B The sapphire was large and shone brilliantly.

C The sapphire came from a place near the sea.

D The sapphire was shaped like the sea.

7 The narrator says the Sphinx is "as old as the world itself." This means the Sphinx is—

A gray-haired.

B all-knowing.

C ancient.

D sophisticated.

8 What is the theme of the passage? Use textual evidence to support your thoughts about the theme. (3 points)

_____

_____

_____

_____

_____

_____

_____

_____

_____

_____

_____

_____

_____

9 The writer uses words and phrases such as *starving children, suffering,* and *poor* to create a—

A cautious tone.

B sympathetic tone.

C earnest tone.

D soothing tone.

10 Icicles that are "like crystal daggers" are probably—

A cold.

B breakable.

C sharp and pointed.

D icy and shiny.

GO ON

Reading Literature Lesson 4

Structure

Review the Standards (RL.9.5)

• Analyze how **structure** contributes to meaning and style

Q: What is the **structure** of a text?

A: Structure refers to how a work is organized. A story's structure is how the plot is arranged. When reading a story, consider the order of events including the rising action, climax, and denouement, or ending. The structure of poetry is how the lines are written and arranged. Some poetry has a structure of rhyming lines in stanzas. Other poetry has no set pattern of rhyme or meter.

Q: How can I analyze the way structure contributes to meaning and style?

A: To analyze structure, ask, *How does the form of the poem or story help me understand the theme?* or *Why did the author organize the text this way?* For example, a free verse poem won't include unnecessary words to establish a rhyme or a certain meter.

The structure of a short story will often have **flashbacks**, or a transition in the story to an event during an earlier time. These flashbacks often create suspense or show important ideas related to the theme. For example, in a story about a man searching for his lost sister, a flashback to childhood could be used to illustrate his bond with his sister. Structure also helps establish a poem or story's style, whether it is formal or informal, complex or simple. A story with an informal style may have a wandering, divergent plot line, whereas one with a formal style would more likely have a linear or direct storyline.

 Try It

Directions: Read the passage. Then answer the questions that follow.

XXI: A Book

by Emily Dickinson

He ate and drank the precious words,
His spirit grew robust;
He knew no more that he was poor,
Nor that his frame was dust.

He danced along the dingy days,
And this bequest of wings
Was but a book. What liberty
A loosened spirit brings!

When I Heard the Learn'd Astronomer

By Walt Whitman

When I heard the learn'd astronomer,

When the proofs, the figures, were ranged in columns before me,

When I was shown the charts and diagrams, to add, divide, and measure them,

When I sitting heard the astronomer where he lectured with much applause in the lecture-room,

How soon unaccountable I became tired and sick,

Till rising and gliding out I wander'd off by myself,

In the mystical moist night-air, and from time to time,

Look'd up in perfect silence at the stars.

1 The long, unrhymed lines in "When I Heard the Learn'd Astronomer" create—

A an unhurried, conversational style.

B a complicated, rhythmic style.

C a broken, confusing style.

D a slow, monotonous style.

2 In "XXI: A Book," lines 2 and 4—

A repeat the same idea.

B introduce new ideas.

C rhyme with each other.

D begin a new stanza.

3 Compare and contrast the structures of "XXI: A Book" and "When I Heard the Learn'd Astronomer." Use examples from BOTH poems to support your answer. (3 points)

_____

_____

_____

_____

_____

_____

_____

_____

_____

For Example 1, you must think about the connection between the poem's structure and style. The lines vary in length but do not confuse the reader or create a monotonous style, so you can eliminate choices C and D. The varying line lengths and unrhymed lines give the poem no distinct rhythm, so eliminate choice B. **Choice A** is the correct answer.

Example 2 asks you to think about the connection between the poem's structure and meaning. The lines do not repeat similar ideas or introduce new ones, so eliminate choices A and B. The poem is a single stanza; eliminate choice D. **Choice C** is correct.

For **Example 3**, you must compare and contrast the structures of the two poems. A good response includes specific examples from both poems to support your answer.

Good: *Both "XXI: A Book" and "When I Heard the Learn'd Astronomer" are arranged within a single stanza of eight lines. However, the line lengths in "XXI: A Book" are short and of similar lengths, while the line lengths are longer and varied in "When I Heard the Learn'd Astronomer." For example, the longest line from "XXI: A Book" is "He ate and drank the precious words." The longest line from "When I Heard the Learn'd Astronomer" is "When I sitting heard the astronomer where he lectured with much applause in the lecture-room." In addition, "XXI: A Book" rhymes every other line. For example, lines 6 and 8 rhyme the ending words, wings and brings. "When I Heard the Learn'd Astronomer" has no rhyme scheme.*

This is a poor response because it leaves out key details from the passage.

Poor: *The two poems are "XXI: A Book" and "When I Heard the Learn'd Astronomer." They are different because they are written by different writers, and they have different structures.*

Try It On Your Own

Directions: Read the poems. Then answer the questions that follow.

The Piano

by D. H. Lawrence

Softly, in the dusk, a woman is singing to me;
    Taking me back down the vista of years, till I see
A child sitting under the piano, in the boom of the tingling strings
    And pressing the small, poised feet of a mother who smiles as she sings.
In spite of myself, the insidious mastery of song
    Betrays me back, till the heart of me weeps to belong
To the old Sunday evenings at home, with winter outside
    And hymns in the cozy parlor, the tinkling piano our guide.
So now it is vain for the singer to burst into clamor
    With the great black piano appassionato. The glamour
Of childish days is upon me, my manhood is cast
    Down in the flood of remembrance, I weep like a child for the past.

Daffodils
By William Wordsworth

I wandered lonely as a cloud
That floats on high o'er vales and hills,
When all at once I saw a crowd,
A host, of golden daffodils;
Beside the lake, beneath the trees,
Fluttering and dancing in the breeze.

Continuous as the stars that shine
And twinkle on the milky way,
They stretched in never-ending line
Along the margin of a bay:
Ten thousand saw I at a glance,
Tossing their heads in sprightly dance.

The waves beside them danced; but they
Out-did the sparkling waves in glee:
A poet could not but be gay,
In such a jocund company:
I gazed—and gazed—but little thought
What wealth the show to me had brought:

For oft, when on my couch I lie
In vacant or in pensive mood,
They flash upon that inward eye
Which is the bliss of solitude;
And then my heart with pleasure fills,
And dances with the daffodils.

---

5   In "The Piano," the rhythm and the rhyming pattern are used to create—

   A a rhythmic, musical feeling.
   B an effortless feeling.
   C an uncomplicated feeling.
   D a childlike feeling.

GO ON

6 Read the following line from "Daffodils."

> When all at once I saw a crowd,

Which of the following lines has the same structure as the one above?

A *Ten thousand saw I at a glance,*

B *They stretched in never-ending line*

C *Tossing their heads in sprightly dance.*

D *In such a jocund company:*

7 Compare and contrast the structures of "The Piano" and "Daffodils." Use examples from BOTH passages to support your answer. (3 points)

_____

_____

_____

_____

_____

_____

_____

Point of View
Review the Standards (RL.9.6)
• Analyze point of view or cultural experiences reflected in text

Q: How do I analyze **points of view**?

A: Point of view is the the way the author allows you to "see" and "hear" what's going on. An author might use the first-person point of view of a child who may not realize the significance of the events. Or one character may know something that another character doesn't. In response, the reader may feel suspense about what will happen when the second character finds out. To analyze points of view, ask *What does one character know that one or more other characters don't know? Or What does the reader know that one or more characters in the story don't know? Dramatic irony* is when the reader knows something that the characters do not know.

Q: How do I analyze **cultural experiences** in a text?

A: A: Culture is the accepted behavior and beliefs of a particular group. When authors write, they reflect their culture and belief system. When reading texts that are outside of your own cultural experience, ask, *What characteristics seem important to the characters? or How would I act in such a situation?* For example, in Indian culture, wearing white to a Hindu funeral is common.

 Try It

Directions: Read the passage. Then answer the questions that follow.

from **The Californian's Tale**

by Mark Twain

[. . .] "Anything HAPPENED to her? Henry, that's pure nonsense. There isn't anything going to happen to her; just make your mind easy as to that. What did the letter say? Said she was well, didn't it? And said she'd be here by nine o'clock, didn't it? Did you ever know her to fail of her word? Why, you know you never did.

Well, then, don't you fret; she'll BE here, and that's absolutely certain, and as sure as you are born. Come, now, let's get to decorating—not much time left."

Pretty soon Tom and Joe arrived, and then all hands set about adoring the house with flowers. Toward nine the three miners said that as they had brought their instruments they might as well tune up, for the boys and girls would soon be arriving now, and hungry for a good, old-fashioned break-down. A fiddle, a banjo, and a clarinet—these were the instruments. The trio took their places side by side, and began to play some rattling dance-music, and beat time with their big boots.

It was getting very close to nine. Henry was standing in the door with his eyes directed up the road, his body swaying to the torture of his mental distress. He had been made to drink to his wife's health and safety several times, and now Tom shouted:

"All hands stand by! One more drink, and she's here!"

Joe brought the glasses on a waiter, and served the party. I reached for one of the two remaining glasses, but Joe growled under his breath:

"Drop that! Take the other."

Which I did. Henry was served last. He had hardly swallowed his drink when the clock began to strike. He listened till it finished, his face growing pale and paler; then he said:

"Boys, I'm sick with fear. Help me—I want to lie down!"

They helped him to the sofa. He began to nestle and drowse, but presently spoke like one talking in his sleep, and said: "Did I hear horses' feet? Have they come?"

One of the veterans answered, close to his ear: "It was Jimmy Parish come to say the party got delayed, but they're right up the road a piece, and coming along. Her horse is lame, but she'll be here in half an hour."

"Oh, I'm SO thankful nothing has happened!"

He was asleep almost before the words were out of his mouth. In a moment those handy men had his clothes off, and had tucked him into his bed in the chamber where I had washed my hands. They closed the door and came back. Then they seemed preparing to leave; but I said: "Please don't go, gentlemen. She won't know me; I am a stranger."

They glanced at each other. Then Joe said:

"She? Poor thing, she's been dead nineteen years!"

"Dead?"

"That or worse. She went to see her folks half a year after she was married, and [...] she's never been heard of since."

"And he lost his mind in consequence?"

"Never has been sane an hour since. But he only gets bad when that time of year comes round. Then we begin to drop in here, three days before she's due, to encourage him up, and ask if he's heard from her, and Saturday we all come and fix up the house with flowers, and get everything ready for a dance. We've done it every year for nineteen years. The first Saturday there was twenty-seven of us, without counting the girls; there's only three of us now, and the girls are gone. We drug him to sleep, or he would go wild; then he's all right for another year—thinks she's with him till the last three or four days come round; then he begins to look for her, and gets out his poor old letter, and we come and ask him to read it to us. Lord, she was a darling!"

1 The reader experiences the action from whose point of view?

    A Henry's

    B Joe's

    C Tom's

    D the narrator's

2 What makes the ending of the story surprising?

    A the contrast between how Henry acts and how Joe acts

    B Henry's realization that his wife has been delayed in coming home

    C the reader's realization that Henry's wife has been dead for nineteen years

    D the preparations that Joe, Tom, and the others make for Henry's wife

3 In "The Californian's Tale," how do the differences in characters' viewpoints create suspense for the reader? Use details from the story to support your answer.
(3 points)

_____

_____

_____

_____

_____

_____

_____

_____

_____

    To answer **Example 1**, you must analyze the points of view of the characters. The story is told from the narrator's point of view. He knows what he can see happening around him and what the other characters say to him. You can conclude **choice D** is the correct answer.

    Example 2 asks you to think about how differences in characters' points of view, or knowledge, can create surprise. The difference between Henry and Joe is not important to the story, so you can eliminate choice A. Henry's realization is also not very important to the story; eliminate choice B. The preparations the men make are described in the story but do not create surprise, so eliminate choice D. The surprise comes when the narrator and readers realize that Henry's wife is dead, even though everyone has been acting as though she is alive, so **choice C** is correct.

For **Example 3**, you must think about how differences in characters' viewpoints can create suspense for the reader. A good response includes examples from the passage to support your answer.

Good: *In "The Californian's Tale," the first person narrator tells the story. This creates suspense because the reader knows only what the narrator knows, so as the story continues, we wonder what Joe and the other "veterans" know that we do not. For example, when the narrator reaches for a drink, Joe exclaims, "Drop that! Take the other." This scene creates a small mystery as to why who took which glass mattered. Later, the narrator asks someone to stay because the wife won't know him, and then Joe and the others "glanced at each other." This glance suggests that Joe and the others have some knowledge we do not. In the end, the truth that the wife is dead and Henry is delusional is finally revealed to the narrator and readers at the same time. (See 3-point scoring rubric on page 12.)*

This is a poor response because it leaves out key details from the passage.

Poor: *The reader and the narrator have the same viewpoint because we, unlike Joe and the other men, don't know what is going on in the story. Suspense is created when a character knows something another character doesn't know.*

 Try It On Your Own

Directions: Read the passage. Then answer the questions that follow.

The Last Lesson

by Alphonse Daudet

I started for school very late that morning and was in great dread of a scolding, especially because M. Hamel had said that he would question us on participles, and I did not know the first word about them. For a moment I thought of running away and spending the day out of doors. It was so warm, so bright! The birds were chirping at the edge of the woods; and in the open field back of the saw-mill the Prussian soldiers were drilling. It was all much more tempting than the rule for participles, but I had the strength to resist, and hurried off to school.

When I passed the town hall there was a crowd in front of the bulletin-board. For the last two years all our bad news had come from there—the lost battles, the draft, the orders of the commanding officer—and I thought to myself, without stopping:

"What can be the matter now?"

Then, as I hurried by as fast as I could go, the blacksmith, Wachter, who was there, with his apprentice, reading the bulletin, called after me:

"Don't go so fast, bub; you'll get to your school in plenty of time!"

I thought he was making fun of me, and reached M. Hamel's little garden all out of breath.

Usually, when school began, there was a great bustle, which could be heard out in the street, the opening and closing of desks, lessons repeated in unison, very loud, with our hands over our ears to understand better, and the teacher's great ruler rapping on the table. But now it was all so still! I had counted on the commotion to get to my desk without being seen; but, of course, that day everything had to be as quiet as Sunday morning. Through the window I saw my classmates, already in their places, and M. Hamel walking up and down with his terrible iron ruler under his arm. I had to open the door and go in before everybody. You can imagine how I blushed and how frightened I was.

But nothing happened, M. Hamel saw me and said very kindly:

"Go to your place quickly, little Franz. We were beginning without you."

I jumped over the bench and sat down at my desk. Not till then, when I had got a little over my fright, did I see that our teacher had on his beautiful green coat, his frilled shirt, and the little black silk cap, all embroidered, that he never wore except on inspection and prize days. Besides, the whole school seemed so strange and solemn. But the thing that surprised me most was to see, on the back benches that were always empty, the village people sitting quietly like ourselves; old Hauser, with his three-cornered hat, the former mayor, the former postmaster, and several others besides. Everybody looked sad; and Hauser had brought an old primer, thumbed at the edges, and he held it open on his knees with his great spectacles lying across the pages.

While I was wondering about it all, M. Hamel mounted his chair, and, in the same grave and gentle tone which he had used to me, said:

"My children, this is the last lesson I shall give you. The order has come from Berlin to teach only German in the schools of Alsace and Lorraine. The new master comes to-morrow. This is your last French lesson. I want you to be very attentive."

What a thunder-clap these words were to me!

Oh, the wretches; that was what they had put up at the town-hall!

My last French lesson! Why, I hardly knew how to write! I should never learn any more! I must stop there, then! Oh, how sorry I was for not learning my lessons, for seeking birds' eggs, or going sliding on the Saar! My books, that had seemed such a nuisance a while ago, so heavy to carry, my grammar, and my history of the saints, were old friends now that I couldn't give up. And M. Hamel, too; the idea that he was going away, that I should never see him again, made me forget all about his ruler and how cranky he was.

Poor man! It was in honor of this last lesson that he had put on his fine Sunday-clothes, and now I understood why the old men of the village were sitting there in the back of the room. It was because they were sorry, too, that they had not gone to school more. It was their way of thanking our master for his forty years of faithful service and of showing their respect for the country that was theirs no more.

While I was thinking of all this, I heard my name called. It was my turn to recite. What would I not have given to be able to say that dreadful rule for the participle all through, very loud and clear, and without one mistake? But I got mixed up on the first words and stood there, holding on to my desk, my heart beating, and not daring to look up. I heard M. Hamel say to me:

"I won't scold you, little Franz; you must feel bad enough. See how it is! Every day we have said to ourselves: 'Bah! I've plenty of time. I'll learn it to-morrow.' And now you see where we've come out. Ah, that's the great trouble with Alsace; she puts off learning till to-morrow. Now those fellows out there will have the right to say to you: 'How is it; you pretend to be Frenchmen, and yet you can neither speak nor write your own language?' But you are not the worst, poor little Franz. We've all a great deal to reproach ourselves with.

GO ON →

"Your parents were not anxious enough to have you learn. They preferred to put you to work on a farm or at the mills, so as to have a little more money. And I? I've been to blame also. Have I not often sent you to water my flowers instead of learning your lessons? And when I wanted to go fishing, did I not just give you a holiday?"

Then, from one thing to another, M. Hamel went on to talk of the French language, saying that it was the most beautiful language in the world—the clearest, the most logical; that we must guard it among us and never forget it, because when a people are enslaved, as long as they hold fast to their language it is as if they had the key to their prison. Then he opened a grammar and read us our lesson. I was amazed to see how well I understood it. All he said seemed so easy, so easy! I think, too, that I had never listened so carefully, and that he had never explained everything with so much patience. It seemed almost as if the poor man wanted to give us all he knew before going away, and to put it all into our heads at one stroke.

After the grammar, we had a lesson in writing. That day M. Hamel had new copies for us, written in a beautiful round hand: France, Alsace, France, Alsace. They looked like little flags floating everywhere in the school-room, hung from the rod at the top of our desks. You ought to have seen how every one set to work, and how quiet it was! The only sound was the scratching of the pens over the paper. Once some beetles flew in; but nobody paid any attention to them, not even the littlest ones, who worked right on tracing their fish-hooks, as if that was French, too. On the roof the pigeons cooed very low, and I thought to myself:

"Will they make them sing in German, even the pigeons?"

Whenever I looked up from my writing I saw M. Hamel sitting motionless in his chair and gazing first at one thing, then at another, as if he wanted to fix in his mind just how everything looked in that little school-room. Fancy! For forty years he had been there in the same place, with his garden outside the window and his class in front of him, just like that. Only the desks and benches had been worn smooth; the walnut-trees in the garden were taller, and the hop-vine, that he had planted himself twined about the windows to the roof. How it must have broken his heart to leave it all, poor man; to hear his sister moving about in the room above, packing their trunks! For they must leave the country next day.

But he had the courage to hear every lesson to the very last. After the writing, we had a lesson in history, and then the babies chanted their ba, be, bi, bo, bu. Down there at the back of the room old Hauser had put on his spectacles and, holding his primer in both hands, spelled the letters with them. You could see that he, too, was crying; his voice trembled with emotion, and it was so funny to hear him that we all wanted to laugh and cry. Ah, how well I remember it, that last lesson!

All at once the church-clock struck twelve. Then the Angelus. At the same moment the trumpets of the Prussians, returning from drill, sounded under our windows. M. Hamel stood up, very pale, in his chair. I never saw him look so tall.

"My friends," said he, "I—I—" But something choked him. He could not go on.

Then he turned to the blackboard, took a piece of chalk, and, bearing on with all his might, he wrote as large as he could:

"Vive La France!"

Then he stopped and leaned his head against the wall, and, without a word, he made a gesture to us with his hand; "School is dismissed—you may go."

4 In "The Last Lesson," how does a difference in the characters' viewpoints create suspense? Use examples from the story to support your answer. (3 points)

_____

_____

_____

_____

_____

5 Which sentence in the story shows that Franz lives in France?

A *For a moment I thought of running away and spending the day out of doors.*

B *They preferred to put you to work on a farm or at the mills, so as to have a little more money.*

C *You pretend to be Frenchmen, and yet you can neither speak nor write your own language.*

D *At the same moment the trumpets of the Prussians, returning from drill, sounded under our windows.*

6 The reader experiences the action from whose point of view?

A M. Hamel's

B Franz's

C Hauser's

D Wachter's

Test-Taking Tips

1 When trying to determine the meaning of figurative language, use context clues, or other words in the sentence, to help you understand the meaning.

2 For questions involving word connotations, think about what the word suggests beyond its exact meaning. Look at how the word is used in the sentence. Then ask yourself, *What feeling is the author trying to communicate to readers?*

3 Remember that a writer's choice of words can reveal the writer's attitude or feeling toward the subject matter—the tone of the work.

4 To analyze how a work's structure contributes to its meaning and style, ask, *How does the work's form reveal its theme or meaning?* Think about how the sentence structure, rhyme, and genre (type of literature) support the theme. Consider how smaller sections of the passage work together to create meaning.

Go for it!

Unit Two Practice Test   Estimated time: 20 minutes

Directions: Read each passage. Then answer the questions that follow.

---

from Alastor

by Percy Bysshe Shelley

Startled by his own thoughts, he looked around:
There was no fair fiend near him, not a sight
Or sound of awe but in his own deep mind.
A little shallop floating near the shore
Caught the impatient wandering of his gaze.
It had been long abandoned, for its sides
Gaped wide with many a rift, and its frail joints
Swayed with the undulations of the tide.
A restless impulse urged him to embark
And meet lone Death on the drear ocean's waste;
For well he knew that mighty shadow loves
The slimy caverns of the populous deep.
The day was fair and sunny; sea and sky
Drank its inspiring radiance, and the wind
Swept strongly from the shore, blackening the waves.
Following his eager soul, the wanderer
Leaped in the boat, he spread his cloak aloft
On the bare mast, and took his lonely seat,
And felt the boat speed o'er the tranquil sea
Like a torn cloud before the hurricane.

---

from One Hundred Years of Solitude

by Gabriel Garcia Márquez

Many years later, as he faced the firing squad, Colonel Aureliano Buendía was to remember that distant afternoon when his father took him to discover ice. At that time Macondo was a village of twenty adobe houses, built on the bank of a river of clear water that ran along a bed of polished stones, which were white and enormous, like prehistoric eggs. The world was so recent that many things lacked names, and in order to indicate them it was necessary to point. Every year during the month of March a family of ragged gypsies would set up their tents near the village, and with a great uproar of pipes and kettledrums they would display new inventions. First they brought the magnet. A heavy gypsy with an untamed beard and sparrow hands, who introduced himself as Melquíades, put on a bold public demonstration of what he himself called the eighth wonder of the learned alchemists of Macedonia. He went from house to house dragging two metal ingots and everybody was amazed to see pots, pans, tongs and braziers tumble down from their places and beams creak from the desperation of nails and screws trying to emerge, and even objects that had been lost for a long time appeared from where they had been searched for most and went dragging along in turbulent confusion behind Melquíades' magical irons. 'Things have a life of their own,' the gypsy proclaimed with a harsh accent. 'It's simply a matter of waking up their souls.' José Arcadio Buendía, whose unbridled imagination always went beyond the genius of nature and even beyond miracles and magic, thought that it would be possible to make use of that useless invention to extract gold from the bowels of the earth. Melquíades, who was an honest man, warned him: 'It won't work for that.' But José Arcadio Buendía at that time did not believe in the honesty of gypsies, so he traded his mule and a pair of goats for the two magnetized ingots. Úrsula Iguarán, his wife, who relied on those animals to increase their poor domestic holdings, was unable to dissuade him. 'Very soon we'll have gold enough and more to pave the floors of the house,' her husband replied. For several months he worked hard to demonstrate the truth of his idea. He explored every inch of the region, even the riverbed, dragging the two iron ingots along and reciting Melquíades' incantation aloud. The only thing he succeeded in doing was to unearth a suit of fifteenth-century armour which had all of its pieces soldered together with rust and inside of which there was the hollow resonance of an enormous stone-filled gourd. When José Arcadio Buendía and the four men of his expedition managed to take the armour apart, they found inside a calcified skeleton with a copper locket containing a woman's hair around its neck.

1   In "Alastor," words and phrases such as *long abandoned, lone,* and *lonely* seat set a tone of—

   A mourning.

   B panic.

   C distress.

   D isolation.

2   The narrator says the boat sped over the sea "like a torn cloud before the hurricane." This suggests the boat is being—

   A pushed forward by the wind.

   B damaged by a strong storm.

   C lifted into the sky.

   D steered the wrong way.

GO ON

3   Read these lines from "Alastor."

> A restless impulse urged him to embark
> And meet lone Death on the drear ocean's waste;

The speaker's point of view in these lines help to—

A dampen the mood by mentioning death.

B create suspense about the ocean.

C create mystery about who the man is.

D create suspense about what will happen to the man.

4   Compare and contrast the structures of the excerpts from "Alastor" and "One Hundred Years of Solitude." Do the structures create the same or different styles? Use examples from BOTH passages to support your answer. (3 points)

_____

_____

_____

_____

_____

_____

_____

_____

_____

_____

_____

_____

_____

_____

5   In "One Hundred Years of Solitude," which word is used to communicate a feeling of chaos?

A *demonstration*

B *imagination*

C *uproar*

D *resonance*

6 Which metaphor best fits José Arcadio Buendía?

   A He was the heart and soul of Macondo.

   B He was a man with his head in the clouds.

   C He was a rock for his wife and family.

   D He was a rolling stone which gathers no moss.

7 The long, descriptive sentences that make up the paragraph from "One Hundred Years of Solitude" help to create—

   A a poetic style of writing.

   B a confusing style of writing.

   C an informative style of writing.

   D an inspiring style of writing.

8 Read this sentence from the passage.

> But José Arcadio Buendía at that time did not believe in the honesty of gypsies, so he traded his mule and a pair of goats for the two magnetized ingots.

This sentence shows that—

   A Melquíades and José Arcadio Buendía are from different cultures.

   B José Arcadio Buendía wants to use the magnetized ingots to become rich.

   C José Arcadio Buendía is glad to be rid of his animals.

   D Melquíades is a ruthless and shrewd businessman.

Points Earned/Total = _____ /10

Reading Informational Text Lesson 6

Cite, Infer, and Summarize

Review the Standards (RI.9.1, RI.9.2, RH.9.1, RH.9.2, RST.9.1, RST.9.2, W.9.9b)

- Cite **textual evidence** to support analysis
- Draw **inferences** from a text
- Determine a **central idea** of a text
- **Summarize** a text

Q: How do I cite **textual evidence**?

A: When you provide examples and details—often in the form of a direct quotation—from a text to support your ideas about it, you are citing **textual evidence**.

Q: How do I make an **inference**?

A: An **inference** is an educated guess based upon supporting evidence. For example, if someone comes inside and asks for a heavier coat and some mittens, you can use these details and your own knowledge to infer that it is cold outside. The supporting evidence is that the person wants a heavy coat and mittens to go back outside and your knowledge about the weather in the winter.

Q: How do I figure out the **central idea** of a text?

A: The **central idea** is the idea or argument that the passage is mainly about. Most works introduce the central idea in the first paragraph or the introductory section. Then each paragraph in the rest of the passage supports or develops the central idea.

Q: What should I include in a **summary**?

A: A **summary** of a passage should include the central idea, the main supporting details, and the conclusion. Do not include minor details or your opinions.

Try It

From **Bury My Heart at Wounded Knee**

by Dee Brown

By the spring of 1875, tales of Black Hills gold had brought hundreds of miners up the Missouri River and out upon the Thieves' Road. The Army sent soldiers to stop the flow of prospectors. A few were removed from the hills, but no legal action was taken against them, and they soon returned to prospect their claims. General Crook (the Plains Indians called him Three Stars Instead of Gray Wolf) made a reconnaissance of the Black Hills, and found more than a thousand miners in the area. Three Stars politely informed them that they were violating the law and ordered them to leave, but he made no effort to enforce his orders.

Alarmed by the white men's gold craze and the Army's failure to protect their territory, Red Cloud and Spotted Tall made strong protests to Washington officials. The Great Father's response was to send out a commission "to treaty with the Sioux Indians for the relinquishment of the Black Hills." In other words, the time had come to take away one more piece of territory that had been assigned to the Indians in perpetuity. As usual, the commission was made up of politicians, missionaries, traders, and military officers. Senator William B. Allison of Iowa was the chairman. Reverend Samuel D. Hinman, who had long endeavored to replace the Santees' religion and culture with Christianity, was the principal missionary. General Alfred Terry represented the military. John Collins, post trader at Fort Laramie, represented the commercial Interests.

To ensure representation of nonagency as well as agency Indians, runners were sent to invite Sitting Bull, Crazy Horse, and other "wild" chiefs to the council. . . . Louis Richard took the government letter to Sitting Bull and read it to him. "I want you to go and tell the Great Father," Sitting Bull responded, "that I do not want to sell any land to the government." He picked up a pinch of dust and added: "Not even as much as this." Crazy Horse was also opposed to the selling of Sioux land, especially the Black Hills. He refused to attend the council, but Little Big Man would go as an observer for the free Oglalas.

If the commissioners expected to meet quietly with a few compliant chiefs and arrange an inexpensive trade, they were in for a rude surprise. When they arrived at the meeting place—on White River between the Red Cloud and Spotted Tall agencies—the Plains for miles around were covered with Sioux camps and immense herds of grazing ponies. From the Missouri River on the east to the Bighorn country on the west, all the nations of the Sioux and many of their Cheyenne and Arapaho friends had gathered there—more than twenty thousand Indians.

Few of them had ever seen a copy of the treaty of 1868, but a number knew the meaning of a certain clause in that sacred document: "No treaty for the cession of any part of the reservation herein described . . . shall be of any validity or force . . . unless executed and signed by at least three-fourths of all the adult male Indians, occupying or Interested in the same." Even if the commissioners had been able to intimidate or

GO ON

---

buy off every chief present, they could not have obtained more than a few dozen signatures from those thousands of angry, well-armed warriors who were determined to keep every pinch of dust and blade of grass within their territory.

1 We can infer that the miners cared more about gold than who owned the Black Hills based upon which detail from the passage?

A *A few were removed from the hills, but no legal action was taken against them, and they soon returned to prospect their claims.*

B *General Crook (the Plains Indians called him Three Stars Instead of Gray Wolf) made a reconnaissance of the Black Hills.*

C *The Great Father's response was to send out a commission "to treaty with the Sioux Indians for the relinquishment of the Black Hills."*

D *In other words, the time had come to take away one more piece of territory that had been assigned to the Indians in perpetuity.*

2 Based on the information in this passage, you can tell that the commission—

A realizes they must give the Native Americans a fair price for the land.

B wants to make up for past wrongs done against the Native Americans.

C has taken an oath to carry out their duties.

D is made up of people looking out for their own interests.

3 Based on the information in the passage, what inference can be made about how the U.S. government treated the Native Americans? Use at least two details from the passage to support your answer. (3 points)

_____

_____

_____

_____

_____

_____

_____

_____

_____

4 Which title best expresses the main idea of the passage?

A The Fight over the Black Hills

B The Last Treaty

C Sitting Bull and the Commission

D Mining for Gold

5   Which best summarizes the last paragraph of the selection?

   A   Most of the Native Americans did not want to sell their land. They knew about a certain clause in the treaty, so they knew the commission would fail.

   B   A few of the Native Americans gathered to meet the commission knew about an important clause in the treaty that stated that three-fourths of the adult Native American males had to sign the treaty for it to be valid. This clause was important because many of the men were resistant to selling any part of their land, so the commission had little chance of success.

   C   The treaty said that three-fourths of the adult male Native Americans had to sign it for it to be valid. The commission could not bribe and threaten enough Native Americans to make the treaty valid because they could not intimidate all of the warriors at the gathering. The warriors were determined to keep every bit of their land.

   D   A few Native Americans saw a copy of the treaty of 1868. They knew about a certain clause in it, and they used it to keep their land.

   Example 1 asks you to cite the detail that supports the inference that the miners cared more about gold than the fact that the Native Americans owned the land. Choice B is a detail about General Crook traveling to the Black Hills, and choice C is about what the commission was supposed to do. Choice D is about another territory probably being taken away from the Native Americans. **Choice A** is correct.

   To answer **Example 2**, you must make an **inference**. The information in the passage focuses on how the Native Americans seek to protect their land from greedy people and the commission was formed to meet with the Sioux Indians and convince them to relinquish the Black Hills. These details help you infer that the commission members are looking out for their own interests. **Choice** D is correct.

   For **Example 3**, you must make an **inference** about how the United States government treated the Native Americans. A good response includes at least two details from the passage to support your answer.

   Good: *The United States government treated the Native Americans poorly. For example, when General Crook found miners in the Native American territory, he told them to leave but "made no effort to enforce his orders." Thus, the government did not enforce the law and keep the miners out. When Red Cloud and Spotted Tall brought these transgressions to the government's attention, the government sent "a commission 'to treaty with the Sioux Indians for the relinquishment of the Black Hills.' " After some Native Americans protested that the miners were encroaching on their land, the government's solution was to take the land away from the Native Americans. Therefore, the government treated the Native Americans poorly by not protecting their land and by wanting to take it away.*

   This is a poor response because it leaves out key details from the passage.

   Poor: *The United States government treats the Native Americans poorly. They don't pay attention when the Native Americans say people are encroaching on their land.*

   Example 4 tests your understanding of the **central idea**. Some test questions may ask you to choose a sentence from the passage that expresses the main idea or a statement that sums up the main idea. Others, like this one, ask you to choose the best title or an alternate title. The title of a passage should always reveal the central idea. The most important idea in the passage is the Native Americans wanted to keep their land while the government wanted to take it away. The only title that expresses this idea is **choice A**, *The Fight over the Black Hills*.

Example 5 asks you to choose the best summary of one paragraph of the selection. A good summary includes the main idea or event and only the most important details. The last paragraph of the selection is about the treaty and why it was important that some Native Americans knew about a certain clause. Choices A and D do not include all of the important details in the paragraph, and choice C includes unimportant details. **Choice B** is the correct answer.

◎ Try It On Your Own

6   Based upon the passage, we can infer that—

   A gold was not as valuable as silver at this time in history.

   B the Native Americans referred to the president as the "Great Father."

   C the Native Americans wanted to negotiate a new treaty.

   D the commission tried to bribe the chiefs to sell the land.

7   Which sentence from the passage explains why the Black Hills were so sought after?

   A *By the spring of 1875, tales of Black Hills gold had brought hundreds of miners up the Missouri River and out upon the Thieves' Road.*

   B *General Crook (the Plains Indians called him Three Stars Instead of Gray Wolf) made a reconnaissance of the Black Hills, and found more than a thousand miners in the area.*

   C *The Great Father's response was to send out a commission "to treaty with the Sioux Indians for the relinquishment of the Black Hills."*

   D *Crazy Horse was also opposed to the selling of Sioux land, especially the Black Hills.*

8 What information in the passage shows that the many Native Americans had lost trust in the government? Cite evidence from the text to support your answer. (3 points)

_____

_____

_____

_____

_____

_____

_____

_____

_____

_____

9 Which sentence expresses the central idea of the passage?

A Life in the late 1800s was difficult and full of challenges.

B A commission was sent to buy land from the Native Americans.

C The Native Americans struggled to protect the Black Hills.

D Miners moved to the Black Hills in search of gold.

10 Which of the following is the best summary of the information in the passage?

A Once miners began encroaching on their territory in the Black Hills, the Native Americans protested. However, the government merely sent out a commission to buy the land. A huge group of Native Americans gathered at the council, and many were determined not to sell any land.

B After the Native Americans told the government that miners were encroaching on their territory, the government sent out a commission. The commission wanted to buy the Black Hills.

C The Black Hills were rumored to be full of gold, so many miners came in search of it. General Crook noticed the miners, and he told them to leave the area. He never enforced his orders though.

D The Native Americans did not want to sell the Black Hills to the commission. They knew about a certain clause in the treaty that said three-fourths of the adult male Native Americans had to sign the treaty for it to be valid. They knew this would not happen.

Supporting Details

Review the Standards (RI.9.2, RI.9.3, RH.9.2, RH.9.3, RST.9.2)

- Analyze development of a **central idea** and **supporting details**
- Analyze how ideas are presented and connected
- Identify **key steps in a process**

Q: How do I find supporting details?

A: **Supporting details** are the main pieces of information that help to explain, prove, or develop the work's central idea. To identify supporting details, ask, *What information does each paragraph give to support the work's central idea? or What details in this paragraph support the paragraph's central idea?*

Q: How do I analyze how ideas are presented and connected?

A: Authors present and connect ideas in different ways. They may use specific examples or evidence to show a point. Authors may also state a cause and explain its effect, or they may order their ideas from least important to most important or vice versa. Chronological, or time order, is another way information can be presented. The following questions will help you understand how ideas in a text are connected.
What people, ideas, or events are being compared?
Does the author use specific examples or explain a cause and effect?
Does the author order the information in any particular way?

Q: How do I identify **key steps in a process**?

A: The key steps in a process are the main actions that a person takes to complete a process or procedure. A passage may organize the steps using signal words such as first, second, and so on. Some passages use a numbered list or a flow chart that shows the order of the steps. Here is a numbered list showing the process of preparing for a job interview.

6 Steps to Preparing for a Job Interview

1. Review your resume.
2. Practice answering common interview questions.
3. Have one or more mock interviews.
4. Learn about the company.
5. Prepare one or two questions to ask the interviewer.
6. Select an appropriate outfit.

Directions: Read the passage. Then answer the questions that follow.

---

from **Who Was Atticus Finch?**

by Talmage Boston

1   Fifty years ago, first-time author Harper Lee threw a 320-page stone into the ocean of literature, setting off a tidal wave that reverberates to this day. On July 11, 1960, Philadelphia-based publisher J. P. Lippincott released *To Kill a Mockingbird* to critical acclaim and a place atop the bestseller list, where it would stay for 80 weeks.

2   Lee's book won the Pulitzer Prize in 1961, became the subject of a successful movie . . . . (with Gregory Peck in his only Academy Award winning role), and sold more than 30 million copies in more than 40 languages, making it one of the 10 bestselling novels of all time.

3   In addition to the novel's commercial success, the character of Atticus Finch, through Lee's writing and Peck's acting, has pointed generations toward the goal of becoming lawyers—not just run-of-the-mill lawyers, but lawyers aspiring to serve the bar with Atticus-like integrity, professionalism, and courage . . .

4   Shortly after the publication of *To Kill a Mockingbird,* Harper Lee acknowledged that Atticus Finch was essentially a favorably fictionalized version of her father, Amasa Coleman Lee, who married Francis Cunningham Finch. In one of her interviews shortly after the publication of the novel, Lee said she portrayed Atticus exactly as she thought of her father—a man "who has genuine humility and a natural dignity. He has absolutely no ego drive, and so he is one of the most beloved men in this part of the state." Named by Lee after Cicero's friend, Titus Pomponius Atticus, who the author deemed "a wise, learned, and humane man," Atticus and Amasa match up in the following respects:

- Both were small-town lawyers in Alabama who served in the state legislature.
- Both had children who called them by their first name.
- Both were effectively single-parent mentors to their children. . . .

5   The statements and accounts of . . . Atticus Finch . . . throughout Mockingbird establish a Lincolnesque persona in the midst of a volatile, racially torn, small-town society capable of giving only lip service to the concept of equal justice for all. Accused of raping a white adolescent in 1935, Finch's African-American client, Tom Robinson, was not lynched by an angry mob, as he might have been had the alleged crime taken place in the 19th century.

6   Instead, Robinson received a jury trial in a courtroom aided by his court-appointed lawyer, Finch, who,

perhaps uncharacteristically for the time, gave the case his best effort. . . . Because Robinson was black, his alleged victim was white, and everyone on the jury was white, a "guilty" verdict was inevitably reached.

7 Atticus Finch has made a lasting impression on generations of readers and moviegoers. Embracing daily living with the highest integrity, and making the legal profession appear as a career calling of the highest order, Atticus caused many to join the profession. . . .

1 The supporting details in the first paragraph explain all of the following EXCEPT—

   A who was the author of *To Kill a Mockingbird*.

   B whether *To Kill a Mockingbird* was popular.

   C when *To Kill a Mockingbird* was published.

   D why *To Kill a Mockingbird* was written.

2 What is the purpose of the third paragraph?

   A to explain how the book inspired people to become principled lawyers.

   B to explain how to become a lawyer with integrity.

   C to predict the most popular occupations in the future.

   D to describe how books can affect people's lives.

For **Example 1**, you must decide which detail is NOT contained in the first paragraph. Referring to the paragraph and rereading it will show that the only detail that is not included is why the novel was written. **Choice D** is correct.

Example 2 asks about the purpose of the third paragraph. The paragraph tells how Lee's writing and Peck's acting inspired future generations to become honorable, principled lawyers. The correct answer is **choice A**.

◎ Try It On Your Own

3 Explain how Atticus Finch and Amasa Lee are similar. (3 points)

_____

_____

_____

_____

_____

_____

_____

_____

4 The flow chart below lists steps related to the publication of *To Kill a Mockingbird*.

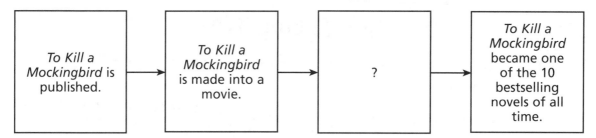

Which of the following statements belongs in the missing box?

A *To Kill a Mockingbird* is about a lawyer named Atticus Finch.

B *To Kill a Mockingbird* is Harper Lee's first book.

C Gregory Peck wins an Academy Award for his role as Atticus Finch.

D *To Kill a Mockingbird* is published by J. P. Lippincott.

5 Read the following statement.

Despite the guilty verdict, the fact that the jury reached it after some deliberation was a tiny step forward in equality and could be attributed to Finch's valiant effort.

In which paragraph would this detail best fit?

A Paragraph 4

B Paragraph 5

C Paragraph 6

D Paragraph 7

6 According to the information in paragraph 4, how are Amasa Coleman Lee and Titus Pomponius Atticus similar?

A Both men had law degrees.

B Both men were admired by Harper Lee.

C Both men were father figures for Harper Lee.

D Both men inspired people to be lawyers of integrity.

7 Which detail from the article best supports the answer to Question 6?

A *Shortly after the publication of* To Kill a Mockingbird . . .

B *Atticus Finch was essentially a favorably fictionalized version of her father, Amasa Coleman Lee* . . .

C *Titus Pomponius Atticus, who the author deemed 'a wise, learned, and humane man . . .'*

D *Atticus and Amasa match up in the following respects* . . .

Test-Taking Tips

1 Go back to the passage to find evidence, such as supporting details, to support an inference or analysis of the text.

2 To make an inference, think about what the text says. Ask, *Which answer follows most logically from details in the text?* or *Based on what the text says and what I know, what can I infer?*

3 To answer questions about the central idea, carefully read the title and introductory paragraph of the text. One or both of these places usually state or give clues to the central idea.

4 When creating a summary, include only the most important ideas or events. Leave out minor details. Keep it concise!

5 Look for how the author orders the information. Watch for words that signal the order of steps in a process or procedure, such as *first, second, before, after,* and *last.* Check to see if the text gives a list or flowchart showing the order of the steps. Does the author use specific examples or explain a cause and effect?

Go for it!

Unit Three Practice Test

Estimated time: 20 minutes

Directions: Read the passage. Then answer the questions that follow.

from The Hot Zone

by Richard Preston

1   A virus is a small capsule made of membranes and proteins. The capsule contains one or more strands of DNA or RNA, which are long molecules that contain the software program for making a copy of the virus. Some biologists classify viruses as "life-forms," because they are not strictly known to be alive. Viruses are ambiguously alive, neither alive nor dead. They carry on their existence in the borderlands between life and nonlife. Viruses that are outside cells merely sit there; nothing happens. They are dead. They can even form crystals. Virus particles that lie around in blood or mucus may seem dead, but the particles are waiting for something to come along. They have a sticky surface. If a cell comes along and touches the virus and the stickiness of the virus matches the stickiness of the cell, then the virus clings to the cell. The cell feels the virus sticking to it and enfolds the virus and drags it inside. Once the virus enters the cell, it becomes a Trojan horse. It switches on and begins to replicate.

2   A virus is a parasite. It can't live on its own. It can only make copies of itself inside a cell using the cell's materials and machinery to get the job done. All living things carry viruses in their cells. Even fungi and bacteria are inhabited by viruses and are occasionally destroyed by them. That is, diseases have their own diseases. A virus makes copies of itself inside a cell until eventually the cell gets pigged with virus and pops, and the viruses spill out of the broken cell. Or viruses can bud through a cell wall, like drips coming out of a faucet—drip, drip, drip, drip, copy, copy, copy, copy—that's the way the AIDS virus works. The faucet runs and runs until the cell is exhausted, consumed, and destroyed. If enough cells are destroyed, the host dies. A virus does not "want" to kill its host. That is not in the best interest of the virus, because then the virus may also die, unless it can jump fast enough out of the dying host into a new host.

3   The genetic code inside Ebola is a single strand of RNA. This type of molecule is thought to be the oldest and most "primitive" coding mechanism for life. The earth's primordial ocean, which came into existence not long after the earth was formed, about four and a half billion years ago, may well have contained microscopic life-forms based on RNA. This suggests that Ebola is an ancient kind of life, perhaps nearly as old as the earth itself. Another hint that Ebola is extremely ancient is the way in which it can seem neither quite alive nor quite unalive.

4   Viruses may seem alive when they multiply, but in another sense they are obviously dead, are only machines, subtle ones to be sure, but strictly

mechanical, no more alive than a jackhammer. Viruses are molecular sharks, a motive without a mind. Compact, hard, logical, totally selfish, the virus is dedicated to making copies of itself—which it can do on occasion with radiant speed. The prime directive is to replicate.

1 The main idea of the passage is—

  A a virus can form crystals and make copies of itself.

  B a virus is a parasite devoted to multiplying itself.

  C a virus is like a jackhammer and a shark.

  D the Ebola virus is the oldest life on earth.

2 The purpose of paragraph 3 is to—

  A explain how Ebola is an ancient kind of life.

  B give the history of the earth's primordial ocean.

  C detail the development of genetic coding.

  D explain why RNA is important.

3 Write a summary of "The Hot Zone." Include the central idea and key supporting details. (3 points)

_____

_____

_____

_____

_____

_____

_____

_____

_____

_____

_____

4 Which statement describes an inference you can make after reading the passage?

  A Viruses are dangerous and uncontrollable.

  B Viruses will soon be able to live on their own.

  C Biologists study viruses to understand life-forms.

  D Ebola has found a successful way to survive.

5 In the process of a virus becoming a Trojan horse, what is the second step mentioned in the article?

  A The virus clings to the cell.

  B The cell enfolds the virus.

  C The virus turns on.

  D The virus makes copies of itself.

6 The author states that viruses are "neither alive nor dead." What information in the passage supports this claim? Support your answer with examples from the text. (3 points)

_____

_____

_____

_____

_____

_____

_____

_____

_____

_____

_____

Points Earned/Total = _____ /10

Unit Four—Craft and Structure

Word Choice

Review the Standards (RI.9.4, RH.9.4, RST.9.4)

- Determine **figurative, connotative,** and **technical** word meanings
- Analyze the impact of **word choice** on meaning and tone

Q: What are figurative meanings?

A: Figurative meanings suggest something other than the literal meanings of the words. Examples of figurative language include similes, metaphors, and personification. To answer questions about figurative language, think about what ideas or emotions the author is trying to convey.

Q: What are connotative meanings?

A: A word's **connotation** is the feeling suggested beyond the word's exact meaning. Although people who are careful with their money can be described as *thrifty* or *cheap*, the first has a more positive connotation, whereas the latter has a more negative connotation.

Q: What are technical meanings?

A: Technical words are used in specific fields or subjects and have special meanings. These meanings may not match the word's meaning outside of that field. For example, in everyday English, cache means "a supply of something." However, in the field of computers, *cache* refers to a place on a computer's hard drive that stores information that can be easily accessed.

Q: How does an author's word choice affect meaning and tone?

A: The **tone** of an essay conveys the writer's attitude toward the subject and the audience. Tone in informational text is established when the author answers a few basic questions about the purpose of the writing: *Why am I writing this? Who am I writing it to? What do I want the readers to learn, understand, or think about?* Tone is a result of **word choice**, sentence style, imagery, and emphasis, among other things. Tone often determines how well an author's ideas are received.

Directions: Read the passage. Then answer the questions that follow.

Four-Winged Birds

In 1915, an ornithologist named William Beebe first put forward the concept that as birds evolved from dinosaurs, they passed through a four-winged stage. There was little evidence to support his view, but a finding in 2003 made people realize that Beebe had been ahead of his time. In that year, Xing Xu, a renowned authority on dinosaurs, found fossil remains of dinosaurs in which the presence of long feathers on the back limbs is very apparent.

For some time, scientists had assumed that the four-winged design faded before true birds made their appearance, but in 2013 Xing Xu found more fossils—this time of early birds—that clearly show four wings. Xu speculates that the second set of wings protruding from the legs probably helped the early birds turn or glide, possibly like a bi-plane.

Other scientists are wary of the assumption that these feathers were used for flight. Some argue that the leg feathers could have been a mere "developmental quirk" and point out that there is no proof that these back wings were even aerodynamic. And if they were used in flight, why did they then eventually disappear?

Xu answers these questions by examining the possible impetus for flight. Tree-dwelling dinosaurs could have developed wings and the ability to fly and glide in order to expand their range. These tree dwellers may then have gradually moved from life in the treetops to life on the ground. With this move, long stiff feathers on the back limbs would have been in the way. The purpose of the front and back limbs might have then diverged, with the front limbs dedicated to flapping-wing flight and the back limbs to getting around on land. Xu explains, "In the early evolution of flight, different animal groups always try to use as much surface as possible. Once the major flight organ is well developed, the animal just fires the other organs."

Xu himself admits that future discoveries of birds with scales rather than feathers on their hind limbs from the same era—about 130 million years ago—would weaken his position and suggest that the four-winged creatures were a side branch rather than the main line of bird evolution. Yet even those who question the use of the back wings in flight are excited by the recent developments and the part they may play in understanding the evolution of bird flight. As paleontologist Mark Norell of the American Museum of Natural History in New York notes, "The origin of flight is not going to come from just one discovery."

1   Which word from paragraph 4 in the passage is used to communicate a feeling of slow change?

2 Read this sentence from the passage.

Once the major flight organ is well developed, the animal just fires the other organs.

The word <u>organ</u> is used in this sentence to mean—

A a type of musical keyboard instrument.

B a body part that has a specific function.

C a means of communication, such as a newspaper.

D an organization that acts on the part of a larger institution.

3 The author says "there is no proof that these back wings were even aerodynamic." This means that the back wings—

A were too big for the bird's body.

B were used for walking, not flying.

C may not have been used for flying.

D may have evolved into regular wings.

For **Example 1**, you must reread paragraph 4 and look for a word that communicates a slow change. The third sentence explains the adaptation of the tree dwellers from life in the treetops to life on the ground as one that happened *gradually*, which implies slow change. **Gradually** is the correct answer.

Example 2 asks you to analyze a technical word. In this passage, the word *organ* does not refer to a musical instrument or any kind of organization, so you can eliminate Choices A, C, and D. The sentence uses *organ* to refer to a body part, so **choice B** is the correct answer.

For **Example 3**, you must analyze how the sentence and its use of the technical word, *aerodynamic*. The sentence does not suggest that the back wings were large or that they were used for walking, so eliminate choices A and B. The sentence also does not mention the wings evolving into regular wings; eliminating choice D. Choice C is the only answer that explains that the wings may not have been used for flying. **Choice C** is correct.

◎ Try It On Your Own

Directions: Read the passage. Then answer the questions that follow.

from Address to Students at Moscow State University

by Ronald Reagan

1 But progress is not foreordained. The key is freedom—freedom of thought, freedom of information, freedom of communication. The renowned scientist, scholar, and founding father of this university, Mikhail Lomonosov, knew that. "It is common knowledge," he said, "that the achievements of science are considerable and rapid, particularly once the yoke of slavery is cast off and replaced by the freedom of philosophy." [. . .]

2   The explorers of the modern era are the entrepreneurs, men with vision, with the courage to take risks and faith enough to brave the unknown. These entrepreneurs and their small enterprises are responsible for almost all the economic growth in the United States. They are the prime movers of the technological revolution. In fact, one of the largest personal computer firms in the United States was started by two college students, no older than you, in the garage behind their home. Some people, even in my own country, look at the riot of experiment that is the free market and see only waste. What of all the entrepreneurs that fail? Well, many do, particularly the successful ones; often several times. And if you ask them the secret of their success, they'll tell you it's all that they learned in their struggles along the way; yes, it's what they learned from failing. Like an athlete in competition or a scholar in pursuit of the truth, experience is the greatest teacher. [. . .]

3   We Americans make no secret of our belief in freedom. In fact, it's something of a national pastime. Every 4 years the American people choose a new President, and 1988 is one of those years. At one point there were 13 major candidates running in the two major parties, not to mention all the others, including the Socialist and Libertarian candidates—all trying to get my job.

4   About 1,000 local television stations, 8,500 radio stations, and 1,700 daily newspapers—each one an independent, private enterprise, fiercely independent of the Government—report on the candidates, grill them in interviews, and bring them together for debates. In the end, the people vote; they decide who will be the next President.

5   But freedom doesn't begin or end with elections. Go to any American town, to take just an example, and you'll see dozens of churches, representing many different beliefs—in many places, synagogues and mosques—and you'll see families of every conceivable nationality worshiping together. Go into any schoolroom, and there you will see children being taught the Declaration of Independence, that they are endowed by their Creator with certain unalienable rights—among them life, liberty, and the pursuit of happiness—that no government can justly deny; the guarantees in their Constitution for freedom of speech, freedom of assembly, and freedom of religion. Go into any courtroom, and there will preside an independent judge, beholden to no government power. There every defendant has the right to a trial by a jury of his peers, usually 12 men and women—common citizens; they are the ones, the only ones, who weigh the evidence and decide on guilt or innocence. In that court, the accused is innocent until proven guilty, and the word of a policeman or any official has no greater legal standing than the word of the accused.

6   Go to any university campus, and there you'll find an open, sometimes heated discussion of the problems in

GO ON

American society and what can be done to correct them. Turn on the television, and you'll see the legislature conducting the business of government right there before the camera, debating and voting on the legislation that will become the law of the land. March in any demonstration, and there are many of them; the people's right of assembly is guaranteed in the Constitution and protected by the police. Go into any union hall, where the members know their right to strike is protected by law.

7   But freedom is more even than this. Freedom is the right to question and change the established way of doing things. It is the continuing revolution of the marketplace. It is the understanding that allows us to recognize shortcomings and seek solutions. It is the right to put forth an idea, scoffed at by the experts, and watch it catch fire among the people. It is the right to dream—to follow your dream or stick to your conscience, even if you're the only one in a sea of doubters. Freedom is the recognition that no single person, no single authority or government has a monopoly on the truth, but that every individual life is infinitely precious, that every one of us put on this world has been put there for a reason and has something to offer.

4   Read this sentence from the passage.

These entrepreneurs and their small enterprises are responsible for almost all the economic growth in the United States

This sentence uses technical terms from the field of—

A business.

B science.

C mathematics.

D history.

5   Which word from the passage is used to communicate a feeling of strong intensity?

A *renowned* (paragraph 1)

B *prime* (paragraph 2)

C *heated* (paragraph 6)

D *infinitely* (paragraph 7)

6   Which word from the passage is a technical term used in law?

A *candidate*

B *defendant*

C *monopoly*

D *marketplace*

7 What is the tone of the passage? Give examples of how the author's word choice sets the tone of the passage. (3 points)

_____

_____

_____

_____

_____

_____

_____

_____

_____

_____

_____

GO ON

Structure and Point of View

Review the Standards (RI.9.5, RI.9.6, RH.9.5, RH.9.6, RST.9.5, RST.9.6)

- Analyze how **ideas** and **claims** are developed by sections, paragraphs, or sentences of a text
- Determine an **author's point of view** or **purpose**

Q: How do parts of a text help develop **key ideas**?

A: To analyze how a part of a work helps develop a key idea, ask, *Why did the author include this part? How does this part help me understand the text as a whole? Does it build on the idea before it? Does it introduce or explain a key supporting idea? Does it give a supporting idea or example?*

Q: How can I determine the author's **point of view** or **purpose**?

A: Purpose is related to why the author is writing a text. Common purposes include writing to describe, persuade, or give information. The author's **point of view** is his or her opinion on the subject. For example, an author might write an article about a singer, and the purpose could be to give information about the singer's life. The author's point of view may be that he or she likes the singer.

 Try It

Directions: Read the passage. Then answer the questions that follow.

from Composition Through the Ages

by Wendy Thompson

Music as a Language

Music as a language is the most mysterious of all art forms. People who can easily come to terms with a work of literature or a painting are still often baffled by the process by which a piece of music—appearing in material form as notation—must then be translated back into sound through the medium of a third party—the performer. Unlike a painting, a musical composition cannot be owned (except by its creator); and although a score may be published, like a book, it may remain incomprehensible to the general public until it is performed. Although a piece may be played thousands of times each repetition is entirely individual, and interpretations by different players may vary widely.

Origins of Musical Notation

The earliest musical compositions were circumscribed by the range of the human voice. People from all cultures have always sung, or used primitive instruments to make sounds. Notation, or the writing down of music, developed to enable performers to remember what they had improvised, to preserve what they had created, and to facilitate interaction between more than one performer. Musical notation, like language, has ancient origins, dating back to the Middle East in the third millennium BC. The ancient Greeks appear to have been the first to try to represent variations of musical pitch through the medium of the alphabet, and successive civilizations all over the world attempted to formulate similar systems of recognizable musical notation.

Neumatic Notation

The earliest surviving Western European notational system was called "neumatic notation"—a system of symbols which attempted to portray the rise and fall of a melodic line. These date back to the 9th century AD, and were associated with the performance of sacred music particularly plainsong—in monastic institutions. Several early manuscript sources contain sacred texts with accompanying notation, although there was no standard system. The first appearance of staff notation, in which pitch was indicated by noteheads on or between lines with a symbol called a *clef* at the beginning to fix the pitch of one note, was in the 9th century French treatise *Musica enchiriadis*. At the same time music for instruments (particularly organ and lute) was beginning to be written down in diagrammatic form known as *tablature*, which indicated the positions of the player's fingers.

1 The author included the section "Origins of Musical Notation" to support the idea that—

A musical notation was developed long ago.

B ancient Greeks created the system used today.

C people have always sung their sorrows away.

D notation is the writing down of music.

2 The author uses the first sentence in the passage to—

A explain the meaning of music.

B convince readers to study music.

C introduce the topic of the passage.

D contrast the positive and negative effects of music.

GO ON

3 The author wrote this passage mainly to—

   A tell an exciting story about musical notation.

   B inform readers about musical notation.

   C explain some pros and cons of musical notation.

   D persuade readers to learn to read musical notation.

4 What is the author's point of view on musical notation? Use details from the passage to support your answer. (3 points)

_____

_____

_____

_____

_____

_____

_____

_____

_____

_____

_____

_____

5 What is one question the article answers by explaining the origins of musical notation?

   A How old is musical notation?

   B Which musical notation system has lasted the longest?

   C What kind of musical notation is the easiest to learn?

   D When did musical notation become standardized?

6 Which quotation from the article best reflects an inference that supports the answer to Number 5?

A *People from all cultures have always sung, or used primitive instruments to make sounds.*

B *Notation, or the writing down of music, developed to enable performers to remember what they had improvised . . .*

C *Musical notation, like language, has ancient origins, dating back to the Middle East in the third millennium BC.*

D *. . . successive civilizations all over the world attempted to formulate similar systems of recognizable musical notation.*

Authors sometimes arrange a passage in sections. To answer **Example 1**, you can use the header "Origins of Musical Notation" as a clue that the section explains something about how musical notation came into existence. Based on the section's description of musical notation, you know that **choice A** is the best answer. The ideas in choices B, C, and D are not discussed in this section.

Example 2 asks about the author's purpose, or why the author included the first sentence. The author does not explain the meaning of music, try to convince people to study music, or discuss the effects of music, so eliminate choices A, B, and D. The first sentence mentions the topic of music as a language, which is the topic of the passage, so **choice C** is the correct answer.

Example 3 asks about the author's purpose, or why the author wrote the passage. The passage gives information about musical notation and arranges the information in three main sections: "Music as a Language," "Origins of Musical Notation," and "Neumatic Notation." These sections explain what musical notation is and how it was developed, so **choice B** is correct.

For **Example 4**, you determine the author's point of view, or what the author thinks about the topic he or she is writing about. A good response includes at least two details from the passage to support your answer.

Good: *In the first paragraph, the author claims that musical notation "is the most mysterious of all art forms." This statement suggests that the author feels musical notation is interesting and comparable to art. The author also states, "Although a piece may be played thousands of times each repetition is entirely individual." Therefore, the author indicates that a musical piece is never the same. Much of the passage is detailing the history and development of musical notation, but overall, the author conveys a positive point of view toward musical notation.*

This is a poor response because it leaves out key details from the passage.

Poor: *The author doesn't have a strong view one way or the other. The author gives information about how musical notation originated. The passage just gives facts about the topic.*

For **Example 5**, you determine which question the author answers in the section "Origins of Musical Notation." The author does not mention which system has lasted the longest, whether it is easy to learn, or when it became standardized, choices B, C, and D. The author does explain when musical notation was first developed, so **choice A** is the correct answer.

GO ON ⇨

Example 6 asks you to analyze the text carefully. Choice A does not mention musical notation, so eliminate it. Choice B merely explains why musical notation was developed, so it should also be eliminated. Choice D suggests that musical notation has been around for a long time but does not mention when it was first developed. **Choice C** explains the ancient origins of musical notation and is the correct answer.

◎ Try It On Your Own

Directions: Read the passage. Then answer the questions that follow.

James Bond (Ornithologist)

http://en.wikipedia.org/wiki/James_Bond_%28ornithologist%29

James Bond (January 4, 1900 – February 14, 1989) was a leading American ornithologist whose name was appropriated by writer Ian Fleming for his fictional spy, James Bond.

Biography

Bond was born in Philadelphia and worked as an ornithologist at the Academy of Natural Sciences in that city, rising to become curator of birds there. He was an expert in Caribbean birds and wrote the definitive book on the subject: *Birds of the West Indies*, first published in 1936 and, in its fifth edition, still in print.

Bond won the Institute of Jamaica's Musgrave Medal in 1952; the Brewster Medal of the American Ornithologists Union in 1954; and the Leidy Medal of the Academy of Natural Sciences in 1975. He died in the Chestnut Hill Hospital in Philadelphia at age 89.

Fictional Namesake

Ian Fleming, who was a keen bird-watcher living in Jamaica, was familiar with Bond's book, and chose the name of its author for the hero of *Casino Royale* in 1953, apparently because he wanted a name that sounded "as ordinary as possible." Fleming wrote to the real Bond's wife, "It struck me that this brief, unromantic, Anglo-Saxon and yet very masculine name was just what I needed, and so a second James Bond was born."

In the 2002 Bond film *Die Another Day*, Bond (played by Pierce Brosnan) can be seen examining *Birds of the West Indies* in an early scene that takes place in Havana, Cuba. The author's name (James Bond) on the front cover is obscured.

7 According to the passage, Fleming chose the name James Bond for his character because it was—

A short.

B suave.

C classic.

D ordinary.

8 What is the author's point of view on the character, James Bond, and the ornithologist, James Bond? Use details from the passage to support your answer. (3 points)

_____

_____

_____

_____

_____

_____

_____

_____

9 The author's purpose in writing the section titled "Biography" is to—

A describe how the name James Bond belonged to an ornithologist and a fictional character.

B give information about the life of the ornithologist, James Bond.

C persuade readers that James Bond was a famous ornithologist.

D explain that James Bond was an expert on Caribbean birds.

10 The author uses the first sentence in the passage to—

A introduce the topic of the passage.

B convince readers to watch spy movies.

C contrast James Bond with Ian Fleming.

D express a point of view on the topic.

11 The author's purpose in writing the section titled "Fictional Namesake" is to—

A list the movies made based on books written by Fleming.

B explain how Fleming chose James Bond for his character's name.

C persuade readers to read _Birds of the West Indies_.

D explain that Fleming was an avid bird-watcher.

GO ON

12 The final section is headed by the phrase "Fictional Namesake". What is the namesake discussed in this paragraph?

A author, Ian Fleming

B *Casino Royale*

C actor, Pierce Brosnan

D fictional character, James Bond

13 Based on information from the text, what are two reasons Ian Fleming was familiar with the namesake for his hero in *Casino Royale*?

A He was a bird-watcher, and he had read *Birds of the West Indies*.

B He was living in Jamaica, and he wanted to use a very ordinary name.

C He only knew Anglo-Saxon names, and he thought they were unromantic.

D He published *Casino Royale* in 1953, and he also wrote *Die Another Day*.

Unit Four Practice Test

Estimated time: 20 minutes

Directions: Read the passage. Then answer the questions that follow.

from The Mother Tongue

by Bill Bryson

Words are created. Often they spring seemingly from nowhere. Take *dog*. For centuries the word in English was *hound* (or *hund*). Then suddenly in the late Middle Ages, *dog*—a word etymologically unrelated to any other known word—displaced it. No one has any idea why. This sudden arising of words happens more often than you might think. Among others without known pedigree are *jaw, jam, bad, big, gloat, fun, crease, pour, put, niblick* (the golf club), *noisome, numskull, jalopy,* and countless others. *Blizzard* suddenly appeared in the nineteenth century in America (the earliest use is attributed to Davy Crockett) and *rowdy* appeared at about the same time. Recent examples of this phenomenon are *yuppie* and *sound bites*, which seem to have burst forth spontaneously and spread with remarkable rapidity throughout the English-speaking world.

Other words exist in the language for hundreds of years, either as dialect words or as mainstream words that have fallen out of use, before suddenly leaping to prominence—again quite mysteriously. *Scrounge* and *seep* are both of this type. They have been around for centuries and yet neither, according to Robert Burchfield (The English Language, page 46), came into general use before 1900.

Many words are made up by writers. According to apparently careful calculations, Shakespeare used 17,677 words in his writings, of which at least one tenth had never been used before. Imagine if every tenth word you wrote were original. It is a staggering display of ingenuity. But then Shakespeare lived in an age when words and ideas burst upon the world as never before or since. For a century and a half, from 1500 to 1650, English flowed with new words. Between 10,000 and 12,000 words were coined, of which about half still exist. Not until modern times would this number be exceeded, but even then there is no comparison. The new words of today represent an explosion of technology—words like *lunar module* and *myocardial infarction*—rather than of poetry and feeling. Consider the words that Shakespeare alone gave us: *barefaced, critical, leapfrog, monumental, castigate, majestic, obscene, frugal, radiance, dwindle, countless, submerged, excellent, fretful, gust, hint, hurry, lonely, summit, pedant*, and some 1,685 others. How would we manage without them? He might well have created even more except that he had to bear in mind the practicalities of being instantly apprehended by an audience. Shakespeare's vocabulary changed considerably as he aged. Jespersen notes that there are some 200 to 300 words to be found in the early plays that are never repeated. Many of these were provincialisms that he later shed, but which independently made their way into the language later—among them *cranny, beautified, homicide, aggravate,* and *forefathers*. It has also been observed by scholars that the new terms of his younger years appeal directly to the senses (*snow-white, fragrant, brittle*) while the coinages of the later years are more often concerned with psychological considerations.

GO ON ⟹

1   How is the information in this selection organized?

    A by problem and solutions

    B in chronological order

    C by topic and subtopic

    D from general to specific

2   The purpose of this text is to—

    A list the words Shakespeare invented.

    B explain how words enter into English.

    C persuade readers to invent new words.

    D explain that Shakespeare was a great writer.

3   Compare and contrast the information the author gives in the third paragraph about words created in Shakespeare's time period to those created in modern times. Use at least two details from the passage to support your answer. (3 points)

_____

_____

_____

_____

_____

_____

_____

_____

_____

_____

_____

_____

_____

_____

_____

_____

4 The first paragraph is developed by—

   A giving examples of words that were created.

   B explaining how Davy Crockett coined words.

   C showing how words are traced back to their origins.

   D explaining that many people wonder how words come to be.

5 According to the passage, a researcher reported that—

   A dialect words often become mainstream words.

   B new words are invented almost every day.

   C the words *scrounge* and *seep* were rarely used before 1900.

   D most words used today have changed their meanings over time.

6 The author's purpose in writing the second paragraph is to—

   A list the words that are now used in mainstream English.

   B explain how words can rise and fall in popularity.

   C persuade readers to pay attention to how they use words.

   D explain that the English language is unpredictable.

Points Earned/Total = _____ /8

Unit Five—Integration of Knowledge and Ideas

Arguments and Claims

Review the Standards (RI.9.8, RH.9.8, RST.9.8)

- Evaluate **arguments** and **claims** in a text
- Identify false statements and **fallacious reasoning**

Q: How do writers use **arguments** and **claims**?

A: Authors write argumentative texts to support **claims** they make. Within the argument, writers use facts and opinions to support their claims. For example, a writer may argue that high school students should be allowed to go home during lunch. In support, the writer may claim that many schools allow an open campus during lunch. She may support this claim with an opinion from a teacher who promotes an open campus policy and a study that shows how many schools have an open campus policy (facts).

Q: How do I know if a statement is false or uses **fallacious reasoning?**

A: A strong argument relies on facts to support the author's position. To decide whether the statement is false, ask, *What evidence does the author use to support this claim? Is the evidence relevant and sufficient?* **Fallacious reasoning** is an untrue or misleading argument. Fallacious reasoning comes in many forms. The bandwagon approach says that something is right or good because it is common. For example, an ad might say, "More than one million people have bought our product." This statement suggests that the product is good because so many people have bought it, but just because the product is popular does not mean it is a good or effective product.

 Try It

Directions: Read the passage. Then answer the questions that follow.

from **What a Young Woman Ought to Know**

by Mary Wood-Allen

If we were wise we would practise the art of deep, voluntary breathing, as a daily form of gymnastics. What would it do for us? Wonderful things, if we may believe the doctors. Even in the old Greek and Roman times the doctors recommended deep breathing, the voluntary holding of air in the lungs, believing that this exercise cleansed the system of impurities and gave strength. And all our scientific discoverers have proven that they were right, and modern doctors have only learned more of the process and added to the wisdom of the ancients. Professor Lehwess says that he uses deep breathing not only as a health remedy but as a cure for muscular convulsions, especially chronic spasms; and he says that he bases his method for the cure of stuttering mainly upon respiratory and vocal exercises, "whereby," he says, "we work on enervated muscles, and make their function bring them into permanent activity and make them obedient to our will." Thus not only will the respiratory system be enlarged and quickened, and the lungs strengthened, but the blood circulation is promoted and those injurious influences overcome which often take away the stutterer's courage for speaking.

Dr. Niemeyer, of Leipzig, urges breathing in these words: "Prize air; use good, pure air; breathe fresh air in your room by night and day." Dr. Bicking says that respiratory gymnastics are the only effectual remedy for pulmonary affection, especially for consumption. The Marquise Ciccolina claims that by the teaching of breathing gymnastics she has cured people of a tendency to take cold easily; she has benefited cases of lung and heart trouble, and she has cured nervous asthma even in cases that have lasted from childhood to maturity. Dr. Kitchen asserts that if the various structures of the body, including the lungs, are in a sufficiently healthy state, consumption cannot find a soil in which to commence its ravages, or, if already commenced, can be cured by attention to the general health, by pure air and deep breathing.

All this proves that the breathing is of great importance—of just as much importance to women as to men. It used to be thought that women breathe naturally with the upper part of the chest and men with the abdominal muscles, but we have now learned that in the breathing of both men and women the diaphragm should be used and the lower part of the chest expanded. The breathing should neither be thoracic— that is, with the upper part of the chest—nor abdominal. It should be diaphragmatic; that is, with the expansion of the sides of the lower part of the chest, thus filling every air-cell and bringing the life-giving oxygen to the blood. The importance of the diaphragm as the breathing muscle cannot be overestimated. A diaphragm, you know, is a partition across a cylinder; the diaphragm is a muscular partition across the cylinder of the body, dividing the lungs from the abdomen. In breathing, the diaphragm becomes tense, and in becoming tense becomes also flattened, just as an umbrella does by being opened. In fact the opening and shutting of an umbrella gives a very good idea of the motion of the diaphragm in breathing. We can realize, then, how much larger around the body will be when the lungs are fully inflated than it is when we breathe the air out and the lungs are empty. A few minutes spent each day in exercising in diaphragmatic breathing would be of great advantage in increasing beauty of form, in giving strength and power to the voice, in improving the complexion and adding to the health, and therefore to the happiness. In taking these exercises, one should either stand erect or lie flat upon the back and draw the air in through the nose, keeping the mouth closed. Draw in gently, allowing the chest to expand at the sides, hold the air for a little time, and then breathe out slowly.

These exercises performed in a room that is well ventilated, or, better still, in the pure air of outdoors, will do much toward driving away headaches, clearing the brain, giving better judgment, stronger will, and a clearer, happier, brighter disposition.

1   Which statement best describes the author's central claim?

    A Deep breathing cures asthma.

    B Deep breathing has many health benefits.

    C It is important to listen to health recommendations.

    D Doctors recommend breathing with the diaphragm.

2   Which statement from the selection is a fact that supports the author's argument in favor of doing breathing exercises?

    A *Even in the old Greek and Roman times the doctors recommended deep breathing, the voluntary holding of air in the lungs. . .*

    B *All this proves that the breathing is of great importance—of just as much importance to women as to men.*

    C *It used to be thought that women breathe naturally with the upper part of the chest and men with the abdominal muscles.*

    D *We can realize, then, how much larger around the body will be when the lungs are fully inflated than it is when we breathe the air out and the lungs are empty.*

3   The writer claims, "The importance of the diaphragm as the breathing muscle cannot be overestimated." Explain whether the author gives relevant evidence to support this claim. (3 points)

_____

_____

_____

_____

_____

_____

_____

_____

Example 1 asks you to identify the writer's central claim. In this selection, the author is clearly arguing in favor of deep breathing exercises. Choices A and D are too narrow, and choice C is too broad to be the central claim. The only statement that sums up the author's position on the issue is choice B, *Deep breathing has many health benefits.* **Choice B** is the correct answer.

To answer **Example 2**, you must identify factual evidence that supports the author's argument. The correct answer must first be a fact rather than an opinion. When you look at the answer choices, you see that choice B is an opinion, so eliminate choice B. So the next step is deciding which fact supports an argument in favor of doing breathing exercises. The only choice that makes sense is A. The fact that Greek and Roman doctors also recommended deep breathing exercises helps to support the argument that deep breathing exercises are beneficial. **Choice A** is correct.

For **Example 3,** you must evaluate whether the evidence provided is relevant to the following claim: "The importance of the diaphragm as the breathing muscle cannot be overestimated." A good response includes at least two examples from the passage to support your answer.

Good: *The writer claims that the diaphragm is an important breathing muscle. The writer supports this claim by describing how a diaphragm works, saying that diaphragmatic breathing is "the expansion of the sides of the lower part of the chest." The author also mentions that this breathing brings "the life-giving oxygen to the blood." These facts support the claim that the diaphragm plays such an important role in breathing. The comparison of the diaphragm to an umbrella provides readers a visual of how the diaphragm works: "the opening and shutting of an umbrella gives a very good idea of the motion of the diaphragm in breathing." The author uses facts and a comparison to provide evidence of how important the diaphragm is to breathing.*

This is a poor response because it doesn't evaluate specific evidence that supports the claim.

Poor: *The writer claims, "The importance of the diaphragm as the breathing muscle cannot be overestimated." The diaphragm is an integral part of breathing, and the author does a good job of creating support for her viewpoint.*

◎ Try It On Your Own

---

4   Read this statement from the selection.

If we were wise we would practise the art of deep, voluntary breathing, as a daily form of gymnastics.

The writer uses the word <u>art</u> to—

A show how gymnastics is a creative sport.

B draw attention to irrelevant information.

C point out how people can improve their breathing.

D associate a positive connotation with deep-breathing exercises.

5 Give two details from the passage that supports the author's claim that deep breathing is beneficial. Do you think the author provides sufficient evidence to support the claim. (3 points)

_____

_____

_____

_____

_____

_____

_____

_____

_____

6 Which detail from the passage is most relevant to understanding why doctors think deep breathing has health benefits?

A *If we were wise we would practise the art of deep, voluntary breathing . . .*

B *Wonderful things, if we may believe the doctors.*

C *. . . modern doctors have only learned more of the process and added to the wisdom of the ancients.*

D *. . . by the teaching of breathing gymnastics she has cured people of a tendency to take cold easily . . .*

7 Which statement is an opinion?

A *In breathing, the diaphragm becomes tense, and in becoming tense becomes also flattened. . .*

B *. . .the diaphragm is a muscular partition across the cylinder of the body, dividing the lungs from the abdomen.*

C *Draw in gently, allowing the chest to expand at the sides, hold the air for a little time, and then breathe out slowly.*

D *These exercises . . . will do much toward . . . giving better judgment, stronger will, and a clearer, happier, brighter disposition.*

U.S. Documents

Review the Standards (RI.9.9)

• Analyze documents of **historical and literary significance**

• Identify how documents address related themes and concepts

Q: How do I analyze documents of **historical and literary significance**?

A: When reading documents with **historical and literary significance**, think about the time period in which they were written to provide context. Ask questions such as, *Does the work describe an important event in history? How does the time period affect the work?* Then think about the literary significance, such as the themes, author's purpose and text structure, as well as other literary elements.

Q: How do documents address related themes and concepts?

A: When considering how documents address related themes and concepts, think about the time period in which they were written. Ask yourself, *What was a major event of the time period? What historical events were taking place? What kinds of changes were taking place in the country?* U.S. documents written around the time of the Civil War would most likely address the theme of slavery. Slavery divided the United States and led to the Civil War, so historical documents of this time would focus on this major historical theme. One way a historical document might address the theme of slavery would be to point out the inhumanity of its practice and petition for its abolishment.

 Try It

Directions: Read each passage. Then answer the questions that follow.

The Gettysburg Address

by Abraham Lincoln

Gettysburg, Pennsylvania, November 19, 1863

Four score and seven years ago our fathers brought forth upon this continent, a new nation, conceived in liberty, and dedicated to the proposition that all men are created equal.

Now we are engaged in a great civil war, testing whether that nation, or any nation so conceived and so dedicated, can long endure. We are met on a great

GO ON

battlefield of that war. We have come to dedicate a portion of that field, as a final resting place for those who here gave their lives that that nation might live. It is altogether fitting and proper that we should do this.

But, in a larger sense, we can not dedicate—we can not consecrate—we can not hallow—this ground. The brave men, living and dead, who struggled here have consecrated it, far above our poor power to add or detract. The world will little note, nor long remember what we say here, but it can never forget what they did here. It is for us the living, rather, to be dedicated here to the unfinished work which they who fought here have thus far so nobly advanced. It is rather for us to be here dedicated to the great task remaining before us—that from these honored dead we take increased devotion to that cause for which they gave the last full measure of devotion—that we here highly resolve that these dead shall not have died in vain—that this nation, under God, shall have a new birth of freedom—and that government of the people, by the people, and for the people, shall not perish from the earth.

from Franklin D. Roosevelt's State of the Union Address, or Four Freedoms Speech

1   When our enemies challenged our country to stand up and fight, they challenged each and every one of us. And each and every one of us has accepted the challenge—for himself and for his Nation.

2   There were only some 400 United States Marines who in the heroic and historic defense of Wake Island inflicted such great losses on the enemy. Some of those men were killed in action; and others are now prisoners of war. When the survivors of that great fight are liberated and restored to their homes, they will learn that a hundred and thirty million of their fellow citizens have been inspired to render their own full share of service and sacrifice.

3   We can well say that our men on the fighting fronts have already proved that Americans today are just as rugged and just as tough as any of the heroes whose exploits we celebrate on the Fourth of July.

4   Many people ask, "When will this war end?" There is only one answer to that. It will end just as soon as we make it end, by our combined efforts, our combined strength, our combined determination to fight through and work through until the end—the end of militarism in Germany and Italy and Japan. Most certainly we shall not settle for less.

5   That is the spirit in which discussions have been conducted during the visit of the British Prime Minister to Washington. Mr. Churchill and I understand each other, our motives and our purposes. Together, during the past two weeks, we have faced squarely the major military and economic problems of this greatest world war.

6   All in our Nation have been cheered by Mr. Churchill's visit. We have been deeply stirred by his great message to us. He is welcome in our midst, and we unite in wishing him a safe return to his home.

7   For we are fighting on the same side with the British people, who fought alone for long, terrible months, and withstood the enemy with fortitude and tenacity and skill.

8   We are fighting on the same side with the Russian people who have seen the Nazi hordes swarm up to the very gates of Moscow, and who with almost superhuman will and courage have forced the invaders back into retreat.

9   We are fighting on the same side as the brave people of China—those millions who for four and a half long years have withstood bombs and starvation and have whipped the invaders time and again in spite of the superior Japanese equipment and arms. Yes, we are fighting on the same side as the indomitable Dutch. We are fighting on the same side as all the other Governments in exile, whom Hitler and all his armies and all his Gestapo have not been able to conquer.

10   But we of the United Nations are not making all this sacrifice of human effort and human lives to return to the kind of world we had after the last world war.

11   We are fighting today for security, for progress, and for peace, not only for ourselves but for all men, not only for one generation but for all generations. We are fighting to cleanse the world of ancient evils, ancient ills.

12   Our enemies are guided by brutal cynicism, by unholy contempt for the human race. We are inspired by a faith that goes back through all the years to the first chapter of the Book of Genesis: "God created man in His own image."

13   We on our side are striving to be true to that divine heritage. We are fighting, as our fathers have fought, to uphold the doctrine that all men are equal in the sight of God. Those on the other side are striving to destroy this deep belief and to create a world in their own image—a world of tyranny and cruelty and serfdom.

14   That is the conflict that day and night now pervades our lives. No compromise can end that conflict. There never has been—there never can be—successful compromise between good and evil. Only total victory can reward the champions of tolerance, and decency, and freedom, and faith.

1   Which statement from the Gettysburg Address shows it has historical significance?

A *Four score and seven years ago . . .*

B *Now we are engaged in a great civil war . . .*

C *It is altogether fitting and proper that we should do this.*

D *. . . but it can never forget what they did here.*

2 Which detail from the Gettysburg Address best supports the theme that soldiers deserve remembrance and respect?

A *The world will little note, nor long remember what we say here.*

B *We have come to dedicate a portion of that field, as a final resting place for those who here gave their lives that that nation might live.*

C *But, in a larger sense, we can not dedicate—we can not consecrate—we can not hallow—this ground.*

D *It is rather for us to be here dedicated to the great task remaining before us.*

3 What is a theme present in both passages? Use at least one detail from each passage to support your answer. (3 points)

_____

_____

_____

_____

_____

_____

_____

_____

_____

_____

_____

For **Example 1,** you must evaluate which evidence from the text indicates a significant historical event. Choice A shows only an amount of time, and choices C and D are details that do not reference any particular historical event, so you can eliminate choices A, C, and D. Choice B references the Civil War. **Choice B** is the correct answer.

Example 2 asks you to analyze the theme that soldiers deserve remembrance. You can eliminate choice A because it does not mention soldiers. Choices C and D mention dedication but not soldiers, so eliminate them. Choice B is the only detail that mentions soldiers, so **choice B** is correct.

For **Example 3,** you must write an analysis of how both passages address a similar theme. A good response includes examples from the passages to support your answer

Good: *Both passages show the theme that freedom is worth fighting for. In the Gettysburg Address, Lincoln states, "these dead shall not have died in vain—that this nation, under God, shall have a new birth of freedom." He claims that those who lost their lives fighting have done so for freedom's sake and that they have not died in vain. This shows he believes freedom is worth fighting and even dying for. In the State of the Union address, Roosevelt says, "Only total victory can reward the champions of tolerance, and decency, and freedom, and faith." Roosevelt indicates that victory is the only outcome for those fighting for those ideals, including freedom. With this statement, he illustrates that he believes freedom is worth fighting for. Therefore, both passages mention freedom and the idea that it is worth fighting for.*

This is a poor response because it leaves out key details from the passage.

Poor: *Both passages show that freedom is worth fighting for. The first passage talks about freedom because of the soldiers who died fighting in the war. The second passage mentions freedom as well and how it is definitely worth fighting for.*

◎ Try It On Your Own

4   Compare and contrast how these two passages portray the enemy. Use at least one detail from each passage to support your answer. (3 points)

_____

_____

_____

_____

_____

_____

_____

_____

_____

_____

_____

_____

GO ON →

5 Which statement from the State of the Union Address suggests it has historical significance?

A *And each and every one of us has accepted the challenge . . .*

B *It will end just as soon as we make it end . . .*

C *We are fighting on the same side as all the other Governments in exile, whom Hitler and all his armies and all his Gestapo have not been able to conquer.*

D *We are fighting to cleanse the world of ancient evils, ancient ills.*

6 In the State of the Union Address, paragraphs 7, 8, and 9 seek to inspire readers by—

A listing allies and how they are persevering.

B giving examples of other nations.

C explaining how the Russian people fought.

D naming Hitler as the enemy.

Test-Taking Tips

1 When reading arguments, look for claims the writer makes. Think about how the claims are supported by facts (can be proven to be true) and opinions (expresses beliefs or feelings).

2 When identifying an author's position on an issue or topic, be on the lookout for loaded language. Watch for words with positive connotations, such as *great* and *best*, or negative ones, such as *poor* or *worst*.

3 Watch our for irrelevant information—facts or ideas that do not clearly support a claim.

4 Annotate or take notes on paired passages as you read. Notes will help you keep track of where and how the texts agree or disagree on facts or interpretation.

5 As you analyze historical documents, keep in mind the time period in which they were written and major events that were occuring during that time period.

Unit Five Practice Test

Estimated time: 20 minutes

Directions: Read the passages. Then answer the questions that follow.

from John F. Kennedy's Televised Address to the Nation on Civil Rights, June 11, 1963

Good evening my fellow citizens:

This afternoon, following a series of threats and defiant statements, the presence of Alabama National Guardsmen was required on the University of Alabama to carry out the final and unequivocal order of the United States District Court of the Northern District of Alabama. That order called for the admission of two clearly qualified young Alabama residents who happened to have been born Negro.

That they were admitted peacefully on the campus is due in good measure to the conduct of the students of the University of Alabama, who met their responsibilities in a constructive way.

I hope that every American, regardless of where he lives, will stop and examine his conscience about this and other related incidents. This Nation was founded by men of many nations and backgrounds. It was founded on the principle that all men are created equal, and that the rights of every man are diminished when the rights of one man are threatened. [. . .]

We are confronted primarily with a moral issue. It is as old as the scriptures and is as clear as the American Constitution.

The heart of the question is whether all Americans are to be afforded equal rights and equal opportunities, whether we are going to treat our fellow Americans as we want to be treated. If an American, because his skin is dark, cannot eat lunch in a restaurant open to the public, if he cannot send his children to the best public school available, if he cannot vote for the public officials who will represent him, if, in short, he cannot enjoy the full and free life which all of us want, then who among us would be content to have the color of his skin changed and stand in his place? Who among us would then be content with the counsels of patience and delay?

One hundred years of delay have passed since President Lincoln freed the slaves, yet their heirs, their grandsons, are not fully free. They are not yet freed from the bonds of injustice. They are not yet freed from social and economic oppression. And this Nation, for all its hopes and all its boasts, will not be fully free until all its citizens are free.

We preach freedom around the world, and we mean it, and we cherish our freedom here at home, but are we to say to the world, and much more importantly, to each other that this is the land of the free except for the Negroes; that we have no second-class citizens except Negroes; that we have no class or caste system, no ghettoes, no master race except with respect to Negroes?

Now the time has come for this Nation to fulfill its promise. The events in Birmingham and elsewhere have so increased the cries for equality that no city or State or legislative body can prudently choose to ignore them. [. . .]

I am, therefore, asking the Congress to enact legislation giving all Americans the right to be served in facilities which are open to the public—hotels, restaurants, theaters, retail stores, and similar establishments.

This seems to me to be an elementary right. Its denial is an arbitrary indignity that no American in 1963 should have to endure, but many do.

I have recently met with scores of business leaders urging them to take voluntary action to end this discrimination and I have been encouraged by their response, and in the last 2 weeks over 75 cities have seen progress made in desegregating these kinds of facilities. But many are unwilling to act alone, and for this reason, nationwide legislation is needed if we are to move this problem from the streets to the courts.

I am also asking the Congress to authorize the Federal Government to participate more fully in lawsuits designed to end segregation in public education. We have succeeded in persuading many districts to desegregate voluntarily. Dozens have admitted Negroes without violence. Today a Negro is attending a State-supported institution in every one of our 50 States, but the pace is very slow.

Too many Negro children entering segregated grade schools at the time of the Supreme Court's decision 9 years ago will enter segregated high schools this fall, having suffered a loss which can never be restored. The lack of an adequate education denies the Negro a chance to get a decent job. [. . .]

My fellow Americans, this is a problem which faces us all—in every city of the North as well as the South. Today there are Negroes unemployed, two or three times as many compared to whites, inadequate in education, moving into the large cities, unable to find work, young people particularly out of work without hope, denied equal rights, denied the opportunity to eat at a restaurant or lunch counter or go to a movie theater, denied the right to a decent education, denied almost today the right to attend a State university even though qualified. It seems to me that these are matters which concern us all, not merely Presidents or Congressmen or Governors, but every citizen of the United States.

This is one country. It has become one country because all of us and all the people who came here had an equal chance to develop their talents.

We cannot say to 10 percent of the population that you can't have that right; that your children cannot have the chance to develop whatever talents they have; that the only way that they are going to get their rights is to go into the streets and demonstrate. I think we owe them and we owe ourselves a better country than that.

Therefore, I am asking for your help in making it easier for us to move ahead and to provide the kind of equality of treatment which we would want ourselves; to give a chance for every child to be educated to the limit of his talents.

As I have said before, not every child has an equal talent or an equal ability or an equal motivation, but they should have an equal right to develop their talent and their ability and their motivation, to make something of themselves.

We have a right to expect that the Negro community will be responsible, will uphold the law, but they have a right to expect that the law will be fair, that the Constitution will be color blind, as Justice Harlan said at the turn of the century.

This is what we are talking about and this is a matter which concerns this country and what it stands for, and in meeting it I ask the support of all our citizens.

Thank you very much.

from President Lyndon B. Johnson's

Radio and Television Remarks Upon Signing the Civil Rights Bill

by Lyndon B. Johnson

I am about to sign into law the Civil Rights Act of 1964. I want to take this occasion to talk to you about what that law means to every American.

One hundred and eighty-eight years ago this week a small band of valiant men began a long struggle for freedom. They pledged their lives, their fortunes, and their sacred honor not only to found a nation, but to forge an ideal of freedom—not only for political independence, but for personal liberty—not only to eliminate foreign rule, but to establish the rule of justice in the affairs of men.

That struggle was a turning point in our history. Today in far corners of distant continents, the ideals of those American patriots still shape the struggles of men who hunger for freedom.

This is a proud triumph. Yet those who founded our country knew that freedom would be secure only if each generation fought to renew and enlarge its meaning. From the minutemen at Concord to the soldiers in Viet-Nam, each generation has been equal to that trust.

Americans of every race and color have died in battle to protect our freedom. Americans of every race and color have worked to build a nation of widening opportunities. Now our generation of Americans has been called on to continue the unending search for justice within our own borders.

We believe that all men are created equal. Yet many are denied equal treatment.

We believe that all men have certain unalienable rights. Yet many Americans do not enjoy those rights.

We believe that all men are entitled to the blessings of liberty. Yet millions are being deprived of those blessings—not because of their own failures, but because of the color of their skin.

The reasons are deeply imbedded in history and tradition and the nature of man. We can understand—without rancor or hatred—how this all happened.

But it cannot continue. Our Constitution, the foundation of our Republic, forbids it. The principles of our freedom forbid it. Morality forbids it. And the law I will sign tonight forbids it.

---

1 Which statement best describes the author's central claim in John F. Kennedy's Televised Address to the Nation on Civil Rights on June 11, 1963?

   A *The University of Alabama should not be segregated.*

   B *Grade schools should be desegregated.*

   C *The United States is one country.*

   D *Every American deserves the same rights and equality of treatment.*

GO ON

2 Which statement from John F. Kennedy's speech is a historical fact that supports the author's argument in favor of equal rights?

  A *One hundred years of delay have passed since President Lincoln freed the slaves . . .*

  B *. . . we cherish our freedom here at home . . .*

  C *This seems to be an elementary right.*

  D *We cannot say to 10 percent of the population that you can't have that right . . .*

3 Which detail from John F. Kennedy's speech is most relevant to understanding why the author argues for equal rights?

  A *We believe that all men are created equal. Yet many are denied equal treatment.*

  B *This Nation was founded by men of many nations and backgrounds.*

  C *We have a right to expect that the Negro community will be responsible, will uphold the law . . .*

  D *I am, therefore, asking the Congress to enact legislation . . .*

4 How does the author inspire the people listening to his speech to support his argument? Use two details from the passage to support your answer. (3 points)

_____

_____

_____

_____

_____

_____

_____

_____

_____

_____

_____

_____

_____

_____

5 Which statement from "Lyndon B. Johnson's Remarks" suggests it has historical significance?

  A *I am about to sign into law the Civil Rights Act of 1964.*

  B *This is a proud triumph.*

  C *We believe that all men are entitled to the blessings of liberty.*

  D *The reasons are deeply imbedded in history and tradition and the nature of man.*

6 Which statement best describes the author's central claim in "Lyndon B. Johnson's Remarks"?

  A Laws are put into place to protect people's rights.

  B The Civil Rights Act will stop racial injustice.

  C America is one of the first nations to treat people equally.

  D The history of America is full of wars and conflict.

7 Which statement from the selection is a fact that supports the author's argument in favor of providing equal treatment for people regardless of skin color?

  A *I want to take this occasion to talk to you about what that law means to every American.*

  B *That struggle was a turning point in our history.*

  C *Americans of every race and color have died in battle to protect our freedom.*

  D *We can understand—without rancor or hatred—how this all happened.*

8 What is a theme present in both passages? Use at least two details from the passages to support your answer. (3 points)

_____

_____

_____

_____

_____

_____

_____

_____

STOP

Points Earned/Total = _____/12

Language Lesson 12

Grammar and Usage

Review the Standards (L.9.1a, L.9.1b)

- Use **parallel structure**
- Use various types of **phrases** and **clauses**

Q: What is **parallel structure?**

A: Parallel structure is using the same pattern of words to show two or more ideas are equally important.

Not Parallel: Joan likes eating out, fishing, and to read novels.

Parallel: Joan likes eating out, fishing, and reading novels. OR Joan likes to eat out, fish, and read novels.

Q: What are **phrases?**

A: A **phrase** is a group of words without a subject and a verb. A phrase may have nouns and verb forms in them.

Type of Phrase	Explanation	Example
Noun Phrase	A noun with its modifiers Can act as a subject or an object	This room has <u>a lovely view.</u> <u>Two cats</u> ran across <u>the road.</u>
Verb Phrase	A group of words that shown action or state of being	I <u>was strolling</u> near the river. The student <u>has been studying</u> for more than three hours.
Participal Phrase	A group of words containing a verbal that is used as an adjective Modifies nouns or pronouns Usually ends with *-ing* or *-ed*	<u>Dancing with delight,</u> she laughed at the grumpy cat. My brother, <u>hiding in the back of the closet,</u> scared me when I put my coat away.
Prepositional Phrase	A preposition plus a noun	The boy <u>in the red shirt</u> walked <u>through the cafeteria.</u>

Q: What are clauses?

A: A **clause** is a group of words with a subject and a verb. An **independent clause** can stand on its own as a sentence. A **dependent clause** is part of an independent clause because it cannot stand on its own.

Type of Phrase	Explanation	Example
Independent Clause	A group of words that has a subject and verb and expresses a complete thought Can stand alone as a sentence	The puppy chased the toy. The burglar crept into the house and accidentally triggered the alarm.
Dependent Clause	A group of words that has a subject and verb but does not express a complete thought Cannot stand alone as a sentence	<u>After</u> Alicia won the gold medal, she took a vacation. The owners sold the house when the market was good.
Relative Clause	A group of words beginning with a relative pronoun Modifies a word or phrase in the main clause Usually begins with *who/ whom, whoever/whomever, that,* and *which*	The teacher, <u>who everyone likes,</u> is retiring soon. The dog <u>that ate my homework</u> is over there.

⮕ Try It

Directions: Choose the best answer for the following questions.

1 Read the following sentence.

The children <u>have eaten</u> their meal.

The underlined part is a—

A noun phrase.

B verb phrase.

C participial phrase.

D prepositional phrase.

GO ON

2 Which of the following sentences has a relative clause?

    A Walking to work, the banker noticed an interesting thing.

    B My brother studied to become an architect.

    C I need to go to the bank this evening to get some cash.

    D The building, which was designed by my brother, is a bank.

3 Which of the following sentences has a participial phrase?

    A Sobbing over her broken toy, the child covered her face.

    B The child who accidentally broke her toy is sitting in the corner.

    C That child in the corner has been crying for a long time.

    D Well, someone needs to go comfort the poor child.

4 Identify the participial phrase and at least one prepositional phrase in the following sentence.

Tripping over the last step, the man spilled coffee onto his new white shirt.

_____

_____

For **Example 1**, you must understand what the underlined part does in the sentence. The underlined phrase shows the action of the sentence, what the children have done, so it contains a verb phrase. **Choice B** is the correct answer.

Example 2 tests your knowledge of relative clauses. The chart indicates that relative clauses usually start with the words, *who/whom, whoever/whomever, that,* and *which.* Choices A, B, and C do not have any of these words in them, so you can eliminate them. **Choice D** has the clause "which was designed by my brother" and is the correct answer.

For **Example 3**, you must understand participial phrases. The chart shows that many participial phrases have words ending in *-ing* or *-ed.* Choice D does not have words with those endings, so you can eliminate it. Choices B and C have the words *sitting* and *crying.* However, these words re used as verbs, so you can eliminate choices B and C. Choice A has the word *sobbing*, which does not function as the verb in the sentence. **Choice A** is correct.

For **Example 4**, you must identify a verb phrase and a prepositional phrase in the sentence.

Good: *The participial phrase is "Tripping over the last step." The sentence has two prepositional phrases. The first prepositional phrase is "over the last step," and the second one is "onto his new white shirt."*

Directions: Choose the best answer for the following questions.

5 Read the following *sentence*.

When I grow up, I want to be <u>a figure skater</u>.

The underlined part is a—

A noun phrase.

B verb phrase.

C participial phrase.

D prepositional phrase.

6 Rewrite the following phrase so that it is an independent clause.

Eating lunch at the park.

_____

_____

_____

7 Which of the following sentences has a relative clause?

A Many small bookstores are struggling to stay open.

B A haven can be found in quiet nooks in bookstores and libraries.

C The bookstore where I usually buy my books has closed.

D Buying books has become an expensive habit.

8 Rewrite the following sentence so that it has a dependent clause.

I watch my favorite TV show.

_____

_____

_____

GO ON ▷

Language
Lesson
13

Punctuation and Spelling

Review the Standards (L.9.2a–c)

- Use **semicolons** and **colons**
- Use correct spelling
- Use correct capitalization

Q: When do I use a **semicolon**?

A: Use a **semicolon** between two independent clauses that are not joined by a conjunction.
I am leaving; don't follow me.
The weather is pleasant now; however, it may rain later.

Q: How should I use a **colon**?

A: Use a **colon** before a list or quotation.
I am traveling to three different countries this summer: Scotland, England, and Wales.
Professor Collins claims that Lincoln had the most difficult presidency: "Lincoln faced challenges during his presidency which no prior or later presidency had to face."

Basics of Capitalization

☞ Capitalize the first word in a sentence, in a title, in a quotation, and in the salutation and closing of a letter.

☞ Capitalize the names, initials, and titles of people and places.

☞ Capitalize days, holidays, months, and adjectives formed from names of people and places.

> *Tuesday, August 20*
>
> *an Egyptian mummy*

☞ Capitalize every important word in the title of a song, story, play, book, or movie.

> *"Camptown Races"*
>
> *The Adventures of Tom Sawyer*

☞ Watch for short verbs in titles. Even though they are short, they are important and should be capitalized.

> *Nothing Is for Free*

Basics of Capitalization

☞ Do NOT capitalize names of the seasons or directions (north, south, east, west) unless they are part of a proper name or a reference to a geographical region.

We're going to Mexico in the spring.

Turn west at the red light.

 Try It

Directions: Read each question and choose the best answer.

1 Which of the following sentences does NOT use correct punctuation?

   A I have four sisters: Amy, Bianca, Cara, and Diane.

   B Dr. Caldwell was right: "Dancing is about more than following the beat."

   C The chef at this restaurant is amazing, she makes the best desserts.

   D Deke is afraid of flying; he had a bad experience once.

2 Which sentence does NOT include misspelled words?

   A Amelia Earhart was sometimes called "Lady Lindy" because she resembled Charles Lindbergh.

   B She was planning to teach Eleanor Roosevelt how to fly before she disapeared.

   C She liked to read newspaper clippings about sucessful women in predominantly male-oriented fields.

   D Earhart's first women's record was rising to an alltitude of 14,000 feet with her first airplane, which she named "Canary."

3 Which of the following sentences uses correct punctuation?

   A Australia is one place I have never been: it is too far away.

   B I love to travel; my favorite destination is Hawaii.

   C I agree with the professor; "Travel is good for the soul."

   D When I go places, I bring my three cats; Sylvester, Ramone, and Tiger.

4 Which sentence uses correct capitalization?

   A *Thomas is Not my Friend* is my nephew's favorite book.

   B Even though he said to head North on First Street, I headed South.

   C The Civil War was fought between the North and the South.

   D We speak english in the classroom even though many of my classmates speak spanish at home.

GO ON

Example 1 tests your knowledge of colons and semicolons. Choices A and B correctly use colons in a list and to introduce a quotation. Eliminate those choices. Choice D uses a semicolon to separate two independent clauses not joined by a conjunction, so eliminate choice D. Choice C uses a comma to join two independent clauses instead of a semicolon. **Choice C** doesn't use correct punctuation, so it is the correct answer.

Example 2 tests your knowledge of spelling. Choice B misspells *disappeared*, choice C misspells *successful*, and choice D misspells *altitude*. **Choice A** has no misspellings and is the correct answer.

For **Example 3**, you must decide which sentence correctly uses punctuation. Choice A uses a colon instead of a semicolon between two independent clauses with closely related ideas. Choice C uses a semicolon instead of a colon to introduce a quotation. Choice D uses a semicolon rather than a colon to introduce a list. Choice B uses a semicolon to join two closely related sentences. **Choice B** is correct.

For **Example 4**, you must identify which sentence uses correct capitalization. The book title in choice A is not capitalized correctly. Even though the words *is* and *my* are short, they should be capitalized in a book title. Verbs and pronouns in titles, regardless of their length, should always be capitalized. Choice B is incorrect because *north* and *south* used as directions should not be capitalized. Choice D is incorrect because English and Spanish should both be capitalized. **Choice C** is correctly capitalized. The Civil War is a proper noun and North and South refer to geographical regions.

◎ Try It On Your Own

Directions: Read each question and choose the best answer.

5   Which sentence is punctuated correctly?

   A Some people are afraid to try new things, unfortunately, they don't know what they are missing.

   B I tried several new things last weekend: skiing, snowboarding, and snowshoeing.

   C The expert skiers zoomed down the most challenging slope I stayed on the bunny hill.

   D Snowshoeing was my favorite: because I was able to go at a slower pace.

6   Which sentence uses capitalization correctly?

   A The quote was from an article in *the Wall Street Journal*.

   B Weather systems usually start in the West and traveled East.

   C Since my birthday is in december, we celebrate it with Christmas.

   D My parents watched the movie *Up in the Air*.

7 Which sentence is punctuated correctly?

A Dolphins are beautiful marine mammals they live in oceans throughout the world.

B Dolphins may save their energy by swimming next to ships: this is called bow-riding.

C Most dolphins have long life spans; the bottlenose dolphin may live for more than forty years.

D The largest dolphin is the orca, or killer whale: the smallest dolphin is Maui's dolphin.

8 Which sentence does NOT include misspelled words?

A Jane Austen has become a world renouned author.

B Her works have been reprodused both on stage and on screen.

C One wonders how closely her characters' predicaments mirrored her life.

D Her novels create a romantic perriod that captures readers' interest even today.

Go for it!

Unit Six Practice Test

Estimated time: 15 minutes

Directions: Read each question and choose the best answer.

1 Read the following sentence.

Put the certificates in the other envelopes.

The underlined part is a—

A noun phrase.

B verb phrase.

C participial phrase.

D prepositional phrase.

2 Read the following sentence.

She might have been lying to you about where she was yesterday afternoon.

The underlined part is a—

A noun phrase.

B verb phrase.

C participial phrase.

D prepositional phrase.

3 Which of the following sentences has a relative clause?

A Rick, who has a graduate degree, does not know how to drive a car.

B Driving a car can be intimidating if you have not done it before.

C Some people like to drive manual cars, while others prefer automatics.

D This summer, I am going to practice until I am comfortable behind the wheel.

4 Which of the following sentences has a participial phrase?

A The man felt like ordering a double latte, so he did.

B The store clerk quickly mixed the ingredients for the drink.

C The man recognized a friend, and he walked over to say hi.

D Surprised, the woman looked up from her computer.

5 Which of the following sentences does NOT use correct punctuation?

A Drinking green tea is good for health; black tea and orange pekoe tea have benefits as well.

B The most interesting characters from The Lord of the Rings are the following; Gandalf, Arwen, Aragorn, and Legolas.

C Recycling can be easy and fun; click on the link below to find out more.

D I will never forget what my uncle told me when I was young: "Computers are just a passing fad and no one will be using them in ten years."

6 Which sentence does NOT include misspelled words?

   A A fear of hieghts can prevent people from enjoying carnival rides.

   B The airport security carefully screened the bagage.

   C Insomnia is an innability to get enough sleep or to stay asleep.

   D Teaching is a profession that requires patience and dedication.

7 Which version of the sentence is punctuated correctly?

   A British and American English have many similarities, but British English has many words not found in American English: *loo, flat, nappy, petrol, queue,* and so on.

   B British and American English have many similarities; but British English has many words not found in American English: *loo, flat, nappy, petrol, queue,* and so on.

   C British and American English have many similarities, but British English has many words not found in American English; *loo, flat, nappy, petrol, queue,* and so on.

   D British and American English have many similarities: but British English has many words not found in American English: *loo, flat, nappy, petrol, queue,* and so on.

8 Which sentence uses parallel structure?

   A Riding in a hot air balloon is exhilarating, nerve-racking, excited, and thrilling.

   B The advertisement needs to be fun, fresh, and be interesting.

   C Waterskiing and swimming in the lake are popular summer activities.

   D To stay healthy, it is important to eat right, exercising, and sleep well.

9 Which sentence is punctuated correctly?

   A Be sure to book the wedding venue in advance; they fill up fast.

   B The maid of honor may be a family member or friend: the same goes for the best man.

   C Most wedding toasts usually end the same way, "Here's to the happy couple!"

   D The flower girl must accomplish several tasks; walk up the aisle, strew petals along the way, and stand in the correct spot.

10 Which sentence does NOT include misspelled words?

   A Many people are under the impresion that the Taj Mahal is a palace.

   B In fact, it is a mausaleum for the queen, Mumtaz Mahal.

   C Shah Jahan employed architects, masons, and carvers to build the tomb.

   D They did their task well, and the Taj Mahal is an exquisitte and enduring monument.

Points Earned/Total = _____ /10

Language
Lesson

14

Context Clues and Reference Materials

Review the Standards (L.9.4a, L9.4c, L9.4d)

- Determine the meaning of words and phrases using **context clues**
- Use **reference materials** to check and verify word meaning, pronunciation, part of speech, and etymology

Q: How can the **context** of a word help me determine its meaning?

A: The other words and sentences surrounding a word are its **context**. The following chart shows some of the ways a a word's context can provide clues to its meaning.

Type of context clue	How it provides a clue	Example
Definition	Explains the meaning	A <u>convoluted</u> argument is *one that is complex or difficult to follow.*
Example	Illustrates or gives a sample	The <u>cacophony</u> outside my window included *horns honking, engines revving, and people shouting.*
Restatement	Says again with a different word or words	Our meeting was <u>fortuitous</u>. It was *lucky* that we met.
Contrast	Uses an opposite	The telegraph is an <u>archaic</u> technology, while computers and cell phones represent *modern* technology.

Q: What can **reference materials** teach me about words?

A: Reference materials include **dictionaries**, **thesauruses**, and **glossaries**. **Dictionaries** contain the most complete information about each entry word, including part of speech (noun, verb, adjective), pronunciation, word origins (etymology), and all possible meanings.

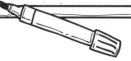

Glossaries are found in a book and contain the definitions of words used in the book.

Thesauruses list synonyms, or words with similar definitions, and antonyms, or words with opposite meanings for each entry word.

➲ Try It

Directions: Read the following passage. Then answer the questions that follow.

Conservative Vice Lords, Inc.

1   From the time of its founding in 1889 to its closing in 2012, Jane Addams's Hull-House was committed to bettering the lives of people of all races and cultures in underserved residential neighborhoods of Chicago. The original Hull House is now a museum devoted to the history of Hull House and of others who worked to invigorate Chicago's troubled communities. In 2012, the Hull House Museum opened an exhibit calling respectful attention to one neighborhood effort in the 1960s that involved the transformation of a violent gang known as the Vice Lords into a peaceful nonprofit entity.

2   The turnaround began in the mid-1960s when gang member Bobby Gore set his thoughts on building a community where aspiring young people could expect more than crime and prison. The Vice Lords were considered the most violent gang in Chicago at that time, but under Gore's influence, the gang changed its name to Conservative Vice Lords and changed its focus to pro-social values and community activism. Gore became the spokesman for the gang, and in 1967 Dartmouth graduate David Dawley, a former Peace Corps volunteer and a person of high <u>integrity</u>, joined the effort to help transform the gang into a respectable nonprofit. His efforts helped the gang boost its reputation and even <u>secure</u> hundreds of thousands of dollars in grant money. With this money, the Conservative Vice Lords, Inc. opened a business office and started several <u>enterprises</u> where neighborhood residents could go for safe, healthy activities: an ice cream parlor, an art studio, and "Teen Town," a recreation center. A spirit of optimism seemed to animate the neighborhood. Dawley moved back to the East Coast, feeling that he had helped set in motion a positive force for change. He wrote a book about his experiences, *A Nation of Lords,* and shared the profits with the Conservative Vice Lords.

3   Unfortunately, the progress did not last for long. Private donations fell as the war in Vietnam drew people's attention away from neighborhood revitalization. In 1969, Bobby Gore was alleged to have murdered a man and was brought to trial. He consistently denied responsibility, but a guilty verdict from an all-white jury sent him to Stateville Prison, where he was confined for more than a decade. After his release, he returned to Lawndale from time to time, where he hoped his influence as a mentor might inspire the next generation. Long before then, however, the gang had returned to its violent ways. "When I came back to Lawndale after being incarcerated for 11 years," Gore recounts, "I just sat up on the corner and cried."

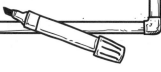

4   The Hull house exhibit was presented in various locations, including one ongoing exhibit in Lawndale. Hull-House Museum Education Coordinator Lisa Junkin explains that the exhibit does not glorify gangs but instead challenges "widely held views of gang members as unredeemable thugs through an untold story of the Conservative Vice Lords fighting for the life of their community."

---

1 The word <u>integrity</u> can be found in paragraph 2. What is the definition for <u>integrity</u>?

A being right

B being calm

C having no doubts

D having strong principles

2 What is the meaning of the word <u>enterprises</u> as used in paragraph 2?

A new ventures

B risky bets

C fresh ideas

D desperate measures

3 Which of the phrases from the passage helps the reader understand the meaning of <u>enterprises</u>?

A *With this money*

B *where neighborhood residents could go*

C *for safe, healthy activities*

D *A spirit of optimism*

4 Which definition best fits the use of the word <u>secure</u> in paragraph 2?

> **se•cure** (sə-kyŭr), [Latin *securus*] v. **1.** to make safe. **2.** to attach firmly. **3.** to procure or obtain. adj. **4.** firmly fixed. **5.** not worried.

A definition 1

B definition 2

C definition 3

D definition 4

5 Which part of the dictionary entry explains the origin of the word?

A se•cure

B (sə-kyŭr)

C [Latin *securus*]

D *v.*

Example 1 asks you to identify the meaning of *integrity*. Use context clues to figure out the answer. Context clues are other words in a sentence, or in surrounding sentences, that help you understand a word's meaning. In **Example 1**, the clue to the meaning of the word *integrity* is the phrase that includes the word *respectable*. This clue suggests that having strong principles is the correct answer. **Choice D** is correct.

Example 2 again asks you to use context clues. From your reading, you know that the paragraph lists "safe, healthy activities," such as "an ice cream parlor, an art studio, and 'Teen Town,' a recreation center." From this context clue, you can eliminate choice B because betting is never mentioned and choice D because no indication of desperation is given. Choice C does not fit since the activities are not mere ideas. **Choice A**, new ventures, is the correct answer.

For **Example 3**, see the context clues you used to find the definition of *enterprises* in Example 2. **Choice C**, "for safe, healthy activities," is the correct answer.

Examples 4 and 5 test your ability to use a dictionary. A dictionary entry tells you a word's pronunciation, origin, part of speech, and all definitions.

For **Example 4**, you must use context clues to determine the definition of a word. The selection says, "His efforts helped the gang boost its reputation and even secure hundreds of thousands of dollars in grant money." The only definition that makes sense is definition 3, "to procure or obtain." **Choice C** is correct.

Example 5 asks about the **etymology**, or origin, or the word. English is a language filled with words "borrowed" from other languages. When listing such a word, a dictionary usually indicates what language the word comes from, along with what the actual word is or was in those languages. The part of the entry in brackets, [Latin *securus*], gives the origin of *secure*. So the correct answer is **choice C**.

GO ON

Directions: Read the passage. Then answer the questions that follow.

Silent Spring

by Rachel Carson

1　We stand now where two roads <u>diverge</u>. But unlike the roads in Robert Frost's familiar poem, they are not equally fair. The road we have long been traveling is deceptively easy, a smooth superhighway on which we progress with great speed, but at its end lies disaster. The other fork of the road—the one "less traveled by"—offers our last, our only chance to reach a destination that assures the preservation of our earth.

2　The choice, after all, is ours to make. If, having endured much, we have at last asserted our "right to know," and if, knowing, we have concluded that we are being asked to take senseless and frightening risks, then we should no longer accept the counsel of those who tell us that we must fill our world with poisonous chemicals; we should look about and see what other course is open to us.

3　A truly extraordinary variety of alternatives to the chemical control of insects is available. Some are already in use and have achieved brilliant success. Others are in the stage of laboratory testing. Still others are little more than ideas in the minds of imaginative scientists, waiting for the opportunity to put them to the test. All have this in common: they are biological solutions, based on understanding of the living organisms they seek to control, and of the whole fabric of life to which these organisms belong. Specialists representing various areas of the vast field of biology are <u>contributing</u>—entomologists, pathologists, geneticists, physiologists, biochemists, ecologists—all pouring their knowledge and their creative inspirations into the formation of a new science of biotic controls.

4　"Any science may be likened to a river," says a Johns Hopkins biologist, Professor Carl P. Swanson. "It has its obscure and unpretentious beginning; its quiet stretches as well as its rapids; its periods of drought as well as of fullness. It gathers momentum with the work of many investigators and as it is fed by other streams of thought, it is deepened and broadened by the concepts and generalizations that are gradually evolved."

5　So it is with the science of biological control in its modern sense. In America it had its obscure beginnings a century ago with the first attempts to introduce natural enemies of insects that were proving troublesome to farmers, an effort that sometimes moved slowly or not at all, but now and again gathered speed and momentum under the impetus of an outstanding success. It had its period of drought when workers in applied entomology, dazzled by the spectacular new insecticides of the 1940's, turned their backs on all biological methods and set foot on "the treadmill of chemical control." But the goal of an insect-free world continued to recede. Now at last, as it has become apparent that the heedless and unrestrained use of chemicals is a greater menace to ourselves than to the targets, the river which is the science of biotic control flows again, fed by new streams of thought.

6 Read the thesaurus entry.

> RECEDE
> *verb*
> **depart**   to leave from a place. *The couple departed from the restaurant.*
> **diminish**   to make or become smaller. *My enthusiasm began to diminish as I realized how much work was involved.*
> **retire**   to go away to a place of privacy. *The student wanted to a retire to a less chaotic place to finish her homework.*
> **retract**   to withdraw a statement. *The senator wishes to retract his remarks from his speech.*

Which synonym is the best replacement for <u>recede</u> in paragraph 5?

A depart

B diminish

C retire

D retract

7 Which of the phrases from the passage helps the reader understand the meaning of <u>contributing</u>?

A *the whole fabric of life to which these organisms belong*

B *the vast field of biology*

C *all pouring their knowledge and their creative inspirations into*

D *a new science of biotic controls*

8 The word <u>diverge</u> can be found in paragraph 1. What is a synonym for <u>diverge</u>?

A separate

B conform

C ramble

D vary

9 Which of the following sentences uses the word <u>unrestrained</u> correctly?

A The tiny princess used her unrestrained, soothing voice to calm the room.

B The scientist searched for unrestrained funding for his experiments.

C His unrestrained punishment was to write a ten-page essay about justice.

D The wind caused locks of her unrestrained hair to blow across her face.

GO ON

Language
Lesson
15

Word Patterns and Relationships

Review the Standards (L.9.4b)

- Use **patterns** of word changes to determine meanings and parts of speech
- Use relationships between words to understand both words

Q: How can word change patterns help me figure out word meanings and parts of speech?

A: Many words in English follow certain patterns. Analyzing these patterns can help you understand word meanings and parts of speech. For example, the word *analyze* is a verb. *Analysis* is a noun, and *analytical* is an adjective. Other words may follow the same pattern of *-yze* indicating a verb, *-sis* a noun, and *-ical* an adjective. For example, *paralyze* is a verb. *Paralysis* is a noun, and *paralytic* can be an adjective or noun. The words *synthesize*, *synthesis*, and *synthetic* follow a similar pattern. Analyzing word patterns can help you determine what part of speech it is, and knowing what part of speech a word is helps you understand its meaning.

Q: How can I determine the relationships between words?

A: Look at the following words pairs, or word analogies.

CHILD : ADULT :: lamb : sheep

The above example reads "Child is to adult as lamb is to sheep." In other words, the word *child* has the same relationship to the word *adult* as the word *lamb* has to the word *sheep*. To answer analogy questions, try to figure out the relationship between the first two words. Then read the answer choices and find the word that most closely matches the relationship of the first two words. In this example, we understand that a child grows into an adult, and a lamb grows into a sheep.

Common Types of Analogies	
Analogy	**Example**
cause : effect	cold : frostbite
word : synonym	mistake : error
word : antonym	strong : weak
part : whole	nose : face
item : category	carrot : vegetable

Directions: Read the passage. Then answer the questions that follow.

A Great Friendship

Sitting Bull (c. 1831–December 15, 1890), chief of the Lakota, refused to live on a reservation. After such "free" Native Americans were labeled "hostiles" by the U.S. government, and therefore subject to arrest or worse, Sitting Bull led a group of about 5,000 into Saskatchewan in Canada.

Sitting Bull was the most powerful Native American in North America at the time because of his leadership in the defeat of General Custer at the Battle of the Little Bighorn in 1876. Sitting Bull had developed an alliance between the Lakota and Cheyenne so their numbers would be strong. Before the battle he had a vision that the united Native Americans would kill their enemies "like grasshoppers." His vision <u>inspired</u> the warriors who carried out a crushing victory over the U.S. soldiers.

When the Canadian government learned of Sitting Bull's arrival, it dispatched officer James Morrow Walsh of the North-West Mounted Police to watch over the camp and make sure no trouble broke out. Walsh had previously been appointed to the post of superintendent of a nearby fort, and he was known for his fair-minded <u>interactions</u> with Canadian Native Americans. He did not want the Native Americans to <u>perceive</u> him and his men as enemies, so when he established Fort Walsh, as he named it, he located it in a valley so it could be in full view of the Native Americans who lived nearby. In this way, when the Mounties went out on reconnaissance, the Native Americans could see their every move and not become suspicious.

Walsh decided to "drop in" on Sitting Bull to introduce himself. With only six men accompanying him, Walsh rode into Sitting Bull's encampment of 1,000 warriors. Sitting Bull was immediately taken by the confident <u>visage</u> of this man and his bravery at coming into an encampment where he was so outnumbered. Sitting Bull, however, did not <u>intimidate</u> Walsh. In his fair-minded way, Walsh <u>apprised</u> Sitting Bull of his intention to enforce the laws of Canada. "People who break laws in this land," Walsh said, "whether they be whites, blacks, or browns, will not escape punishment." Sitting Bull laughed at the idea of a man with only six supporters trying to tell him and his 1,000 warriors what to do. Yet he consented to a meeting between Walsh and the entire Lakota council so Walsh could explain the laws of the land.

From that first meeting, the <u>mutual</u> respect between Walsh and Sitting Bull never wavered. They developed a close friendship, even though they also had heated arguments. When Walsh was transferred to a faraway post, Sitting Bull paid him a last visit, and, as a sign of his respect, gave him the headdress he had received when he had become chief. Sitting Bull and the 230 people who still remained with him returned to the United States in 1881. Against promises, Sitting Bull was later arrested and died in a gunfight that broke out when the police used force to remove him. Walsh resigned from the Mounties a few years later.

1   Knowing that the words <u>reservation</u> and <u>conversation</u> are nouns helps you understand that the word <u>interactions</u> is—

   A a verb.

   B an adverb.

   C an adjective.

   D a noun.

2   <u>Aspired</u> is a verb and <u>aspiration</u> is a noun, so which form of <u>inspired</u> is a noun?

   A inspiring

   B inspiringly

   C inspiration

   D inspirable

3   AGREEMENT : DEAL :: perceive :

   A identify

   B claim

   C decide

   D negotiate

In **Example 1**, you must consider the word pattern. Because *reservation, conversation,* and *interactions* end in *-tion,* they are likely the same part of speech. Since *reservation* and *conversations* are nouns, you can determine that *interactions* is also a noun. **Choice D** is the correct answer.

Example 2 again asks you to recognize word pattern similarities. *Aspired* and *inspired* are both verbs, and the noun form of *aspired* is *aspiration*. Thus, the noun form of *inspired* will likely follow the same pattern. Choice A is an adjective, choice B is an adverb, and choice D is an adjective. **Choice C**, *inspiration*, is a noun and is the correct answer.

Example 3 asks you to think about the relationship between words used in the passage. The example gives you a word analogy. First, think about the relationship between *agreement* and *deal*. These two words are synonyms. So, you need to find a synonym for the word *perceive*. From the context, you know that Walsh "did not want the Native Americans to *perceive* him and his men as enemies." Now replace *perceive* with the answer choices and decide which one makes the most sense in the sentence. Choice A, *identify*, fits in the sentence the best and is a synonym for *perceive*. **Choice A** is correct.

Directions: Use the passage on page 135 to answer the following questions.

4 Knowing that the words <u>dotage</u> and <u>carnage</u> are nouns helps you understand that the word <u>visage</u> is—

   A a verb.

   B an adverb.

   C an adjective.

   D a noun.

5 COMPASSIONATE : RUTHLESS :: intimidate :

   A neutral

   B fortunate

   C befriend

   D callous

6 <u>Mortal</u> is an adjective and <u>mortality</u> is a noun, so which form of <u>mutual</u> is a noun?

   A mutuality

   B mutually

   C quasi-mutual

   D quasi-mutually

7 SOLITARY : ALONE :: apprised :

   A informed

   B repeated

   C doubted

   D warned

Test-Taking Tips

1 Context clues may not be in the same sentence as the underlined word. Look at the sentences that come before and after the unknown word too.

2 When choosing among alternate meanings for a word, decide what the underlined word means in the sentence. Then look for the dictionary definition that best matches that meaning. Be sure the alternate word you choose is the same part of speech. For example, in *to conduct*, the word is used as a noun, but in *bad conduct*, the word is used as a verb.

3 Remember that in analogies, both pairs of words need to have the same relationship with each other.

Go for it!

Unit Seven Practice Test

Estimated time: 15 minutes

Directions: Read the passage. Then answer the questions that follow.

from A Doll's House

by Henrik Ibsen

Mrs. Linde: No, a wife cannot borrow without her husband's consent.

Nora (tossing her head): Oh, if it is a wife who has any head for business—a wife who has the wit to be a little bit clever—

Mrs. Linde: I don't understand it at all, Nora.

Nora: There is no need you should. I never said I had borrowed the money. I may have got it some other way. (Lies back on the sofa.) Perhaps I got it from some other admirer. When anyone is as attractive as I am—

Mrs. Linde: You are a mad creature.

Nora: Now, you know you're full of curiosity, Christine.

Mrs. Linde: Listen to me, Nora dear. Haven't you been a little bit <u>imprudent</u>?

Nora (sits up straight): Is it imprudent to save your husband's life?

Mrs. Linde: It seems to me imprudent, without his knowledge, to—

Nora: But it was absolutely necessary that he should not know! My goodness, can't you understand that? It was necessary he should have no idea what a dangerous condition he was in. It was to me that the doctors came and said that his life was in danger, and that the only thing to save him was to live in the south. Do you suppose I didn't try, first of all, to get what I wanted as if it were for myself? I told him how much I should love to travel <u>abroad</u> like other young wives; I tried tears and entreaties with him; I told him that he ought to remember the condition I was in, and that he ought to be kind and <u>indulgent</u> to me; I even hinted that he might raise a loan. That nearly made him angry, Christine. He said I was thoughtless, and that it was his duty as my husband not to indulge me in my whims and <u>caprices</u>—as I believe he called them. Very well, I thought, you must be saved—and that was how I came to <u>devise</u> a way out of the difficulty—

Mrs. Linde: And did your husband never get to know from your father that the money had not come from him?

Nora: No, never. Papa died just at that time. I had meant to let him into the secret and beg him never to <u>reveal</u> it. But he was so ill then—alas, there never was any need to tell him.

Mrs. Linde: And since then have you never told your secret to your husband?

Nora: Good Heavens, no! How could you think so? A man who has such strong opinions about these things! And besides, how painful and humiliating it would be for Torvald, with his manly independence, to know that he owed me anything! It would upset our mutual relations altogether; our beautiful happy home would no longer be what it is now.

Mrs. Linde: Do you mean never to tell him about it?

Nora (meditatively, and with a half smile.): Yes—some day, perhaps, after many years, when I am no longer as nice-looking as I am now. Don't laugh at me! I mean, of course, when Torvald is no longer as devoted to me as he is now; when my dancing and dressing-up and reciting have palled on him; then it may be a good thing to have something in <u>reserve</u>—(Breaking off,) What nonsense! That time will never come.

1 What is the meaning of the word <u>caprices</u> as it is used in the passage?

   A impulsive tendencies

   B quick action

   C strange imaginings

   D selfish thoughts

2 Which of the phrases from the passage helps a reader to understand the meaning of <u>caprices</u>?

   A his duty

   B as my husband

   C not to indulge

   D in my whims

3 As used in the passage, the word <u>imprudent</u> means—

   A undeserving

   B unwise

   C inventive

   D considerate

4 Which definition best fits the use of the word <u>reserve</u> in the last lines of the selection?

> re•serve (ree-zerv), [Middle English reserven, Middle French reserver, Latin reservare] *v.* 1. to save for future use. 2. to save for oneself. 3. to postpone a decision. *n.* 4. coolness of manner.

   A definition 1

   B definition 2

   C definition 3

   D definition 4

5 Which part of the dictionary entry explains the origin of the word?

   A re•serve

   B (ree-zerv)

   C [Middle English *reserven*, Middle French *reserver*, Latin *reservare*]

   D *n.*

GO ON

6 Read the thesaurus entry.

> **DEVISE**
> *verb*
>
> **concoct** to make something up. *The little girl concocted quite a story to explain the broken vase.*
>
> **develop** to change and grow. *Lifting weights has really developed Michael's arm muscles.*
>
> **formulate** to carefully express something. *The student carefully formulated her thesis statement.*
>
> **invent** to create something new. *Someone should invent a new way to tally votes.*

Which synonym is the best replacement for <u>devise</u> in the passage?

A concoct

B develop

C formulate

D invent

7 SERENE : TROUBLED :: reveal :

A conceal

B disturb

C calm

D protest

8 What is the meaning of the word <u>indulgent</u> as it is used in the passage?

A excessive

B selfish

C extravagant

D permissive

9 Which of the phrases from the passage helps readers understand the meaning of <u>indulgent</u>?

A *ought to remember*

B *the condition I was in*

C *ought to be kind*

D *to me*

10 Which of the following sentences uses the word <u>abroad</u> correctly?

A Max and Ruth plan to go <u>abroad</u> this summer.

B The newspaper is <u>abroad</u> and wrinkled.

C America is such a diverse, <u>abroad</u> country.

D We should eat <u>abroad</u> at that new restaurant tonight.

Points Earned/Total = _____/10

Mastery Test : Part 1   Estimated time: 50 minutes

Directions: Read the passage and answer the questions that follow.

from All Creatures Great and Small

by James Herriot

1   The cattle had been herded into the buildings and they just about filled all the available accommodation. There were about twenty-five in a long passage down the side of the fold yard; I could see the ragged line of heads above the rails, the steam rising from their bodies. Twenty more occupied an old stable and two lots of twenty milled about in large loose boxes.

2   I looked at the black, untamed animals and they looked back at me, their reddish eyes glinting through the rough fringe of hair which fell over their faces. They kept up a menacing, bad-tempered swishing with their tails.

3   It wasn't going to be easy to get an intradermal <u>injection</u> into every one of them. I turned to Frank.

4   "Can you catch these beggars?" I asked.

5   We'll 'ave a bloody good try," he replied calmly, throwing a halter over his shoulder. He and his brother lit cigarettes before climbing into the passage where the biggest beasts were packed. I followed them and soon found that the tales I had heard about the Galloways hadn't been exaggerated. If I approached them from the front they came at me with their great hairy heads and if I went behind them they kicked me as a matter of course.

6   But the brothers amazed me. One of them would drop a halter on a beast, get his fingers into its nose and then be carried away as the animal took off like a rocket. They were thrown about like dolls but they never let go; their fair heads bobbed about incongruously among the black backs; and the thing that fascinated me was that through all the contortions the cigarettes dangled undisturbed.

7   The heat increased till it was like an oven in the buildings and the animals, their bowels highly fluid with their grass diet, ejected greenish-brown muck like non-stop geysers.

8   The affair was conducted in the spirit of a game with encouragement shouted to the man in action: "Thou 'as 'im, Frank." "Sniggle 'im, George." In moments of stress the brothers cursed softly and without heat: [. . .] They both stopped work and laughed with sincere appreciation when a cow slashed me across the face with her sodden tail; and another little turn which was well received was when I was filling my syringe with both arms raised and a bullock, backing in alarm from the halter, crashed its craggy behind into my midriff. The wind shot out of me in a sharp hiccup, then the animal decided to turn round in the narrow passage, squashing me like a fly against the railings. I was pop-eyed as it scrambled round; I wondered whether the creaking was coming from my ribs or the wood behind me.

9   We finished up with the smallest calves and they were just about the most difficult to handle. The shaggy little creatures kicked, bucked, sprang into the air, ran through our legs and even hurtled straight up the walls. Often the brothers had to

throw themselves on top of them and bear them to the ground before I could inject them and when the calves felt the needle they stuck out their tongues and bawled deafeningly; outside, the anxious mothers bellowed back in chorus.

10   It was midday when I reeled out of the buildings. I seemed to have been a month in there, in the suffocating heat, the continuous din, the fusillade of muck.

11   Frank and George produced a bucket of water and a scrubbing brush and gave me a rough clean-up before I left. A mile from the farm I drove off the unfenced road, got out of the car and dropped down on the cool fell-side. Throwing wide my arms I wriggled my shoulders and my sweat-soaked shirt into the tough grass and let the sweet breeze play over me. With the sun on my face I looked through half closed eyes at the hazy-blue sky.

12   My ribs ached and I could feel the bruises of a dozen kicks on my legs. I knew I didn't smell so good either. I closed my eyes and grinned at the ridiculous thought that I had been conducting a diagnostic investigation for tuberculosis back there. A strange way to carry out a scientific procedure; a strange way, in fact, to earn a living.

13   But then I might have been in an office with the windows tight shut against the petrol fumes and the traffic noise, the desk light shining on the columns of figures, my bowler hat hanging on the wall.

14   Lazily, I opened my eyes again and watched a cloud shadow riding of the face of the green hill across the valley. No, no . . . I wasn't complaining.

---

1   Which statement best describes the theme of this selection?

   A Animals are unpredictable.

   B Family is important.

   C Take the bad with the good.

   D Laughter is precious.

2   Which character trait does the narrator reveal when he lies on the grass and looks at the sky?

   A an appreciation for nature

   B an ambition for better things

   C a yearning for solitude

   D dissatisfaction with his job

3   Which paragraph from the passage best shows further evidence of this character trait?

   A paragraph 9

   B paragraph 10

   C paragraph 12

   D paragraph 14

4   The word "injection" can be found in paragraph 3. What is a synonym for <u>injection</u>?

   A disease

   B drug

   C shot

   D organism

5 In paragraph 6, the phrase "thrown about like dolls" means—

   A the cattle thrashed their heads around.

   B the cattle easily tossed the men up and down.

   C the men were afraid of being hurt or getting broken legs.

   D the men treated the cattle very gently.

6 The author's choice of words in the last paragraph helps the story end—

   A on a positive note.

   B with suspense.

   C with a surprise twist in the plot.

   D on a determined note.

7 How does the author use the narrator's point of view to create humor in the story? Support your answer with details from the text. (3 points)

GO ON

Directions: Read the passage and answer the questions that follow.

from The Nose

by Nikolai Gogol

Kovaloff, the member "of the Municipal Committee, awoke fairly early that morning, and made a droning noise—"Brr! Brr!"—through his lips, as he always did, though he could not say why. He stretched himself, and told his valet to give him a little mirror which was on the table. He wished to look at the heat-boil which had appeared on his nose the previous evening; but to his great astonishment, he saw that instead of his nose he had a perfectly smooth vacancy in his face. Thoroughly alarmed, he ordered some water to be brought, and rubbed his eyes with a towel. Sure enough, he had no longer a nose! Then he sprang out of bed, and shook himself violently! No, no nose any more! He dressed himself and went at once to the police superintendent.

But before proceeding further, we must certainly give the reader some information about Kovaloff, so that he may know what sort of a man this member of the Municipal Committee really was. These committee-men, who obtain that title by means of certificates of learning, must not be compared with the committee-men appointed for the Caucasus district, who are of quite a different kind. The learned committee-man—but Russia is such a wonderful country that when one committee-man is spoken of all the others from Riga to Kamschatka refer it to themselves. The same is also true of all other titled officials. Kovaloff had been a Caucasian committee-man two years previously, and could not forget that he had occupied that position; but in order to enhance his own importance, he never called himself "committee-man" but "Major."

"Listen, my dear," he used to say when he met an old woman in the street who sold shirt-fronts; "go to my house in Sadovaia Street and ask 'Does Major Kovaloff live here?' Any child can tell you where it is."

Accordingly we will call him for the future Major Kovaloff. It was his custom to take a daily walk on the Neffsky Avenue. The collar of his shirt was always remarkably clean and stiff. He wore the same style of whiskers as those that are worn by governors of districts, architects, and regimental doctors; in short, all those who have full red cheeks and play a good game of whist. These whiskers grow straight across the cheek towards the nose.

Major Kovaloff wore a number of seals, on some of which were engraved armorial bearings, and others the names of the days of the week. He had come to St. Petersburg with the view of obtaining some position corresponding to his rank, if possible that of vice-governor of a province; but he was prepared to be content with that of a bailiff in some department or other. He was, moreover, not disinclined to marry, but only such a lady who could bring with her a dowry of two hundred thousand roubles. Accordingly, the reader can judge for himself what his sensations were when he found in his face, instead of a fairly symmetrical nose, a broad, flat vacancy.

To increase his misfortune, not a single droshky was to be seen in the street, and so he was obliged to proceed on foot. He wrapped himself up in his cloak, and held his handkerchief to his face as though his nose bled. "But perhaps it is all only my imagination; it is impossible that a nose should drop off in such a silly way," he thought, and stepped into a confectioner's shop in order to look into the mirror.

8 Major Kovaloff calls himself "Major" because—

A he holds the title of major.

B he wants to feel important.

C he believes in tradition.

D he decided to join the military.

9 Based on what he says and does, you can infer that Major Kovaloff is—

A pretentious.

B modest.

C considerate.

D garrulous.

10 What is the tone of the story? Give examples of how the author's word choice sets the tone of the story. (3 points)

_____

_____

_____

_____

_____

_____

_____

_____

_____

11 Which summary best relates the important information in the passage?

A Major Kovaloff woke up one morning to find that his nose had disappeared from his face. He had given himself the title of Major, and he had come to St. Petersburg to get a better post. After he saw his nose was gone, he decided to go to the police, but he had to walk there since he could not find a droshky.

B Major Kovaloff woke up after making a droning sound. He looked in the mirror given to him by his valet and saw that he had no nose. He shook himself, but it was still true. He told everyone to call him "Major," even though he was not really a major.

C Major Kovaloff saw that he had no nose. He rushed to the police station. He had to walk there because he could not find a droshky. On the way there, he wondered if his nose was still missing, so he stopped into a shop to look into the mirror.

D Major Kovaloff saw that he had no nose. He took daily walks outside, and he wanted to gain a better post. He would not mind marrying a woman who could bring him a good dowry.

GO ON

Directions: Read the passage and answer the questions that follow.

Annabel Lee

by Edgar Allan Poe

It was many and many a year ago,
In a kingdom by the sea,
That a maiden there lived whom you may know
By the name of Annabel Lee;
And this maiden she lived with no other thought
Than to love and be loved by me.

I was a child and she was a child,
In this kingdom by the sea:
But we loved with a love that was more than love—
I and my Annabel Lee;
With a love that the winged seraphs of heaven
Coveted her and me.

And this was the reason that, long ago,
In this kingdom by the sea,
A wind blew out of a cloud, chilling
My beautiful Annabel Lee;
So that her highborn kinsmen came
And bore her away from me,
To shut her up in a sepulchre
In this kingdom by the sea.

The angels, not half so happy in heaven,
Went envying her and me—
Yes!—that was the reason (as all men know,
In this kingdom by the sea)
That the wind came out of the cloud by night,
Chilling and killing my Annabel Lee.

But our love it was stronger by far than the love
Of those who were older than we—
Of many far wiser than we—
And neither the angels in heaven above,
Nor the demons down under the sea,
Can ever dissever my soul from the soul
Of the beautiful Annabel Lee.

For the moon never beams without bringing me dreams
Of the beautiful Annabel Lee;
And the stars never rise but I see the bright eyes
Of the beautiful Annabel Lee;
And so, all the night-tide, I lie down by the side
Of my darling, my darling, my life and my bride,
In her sepulchre there by the sea—
In her tomb by the side of the sea.

12 What is the tone of this poem?

   A mournful

   B apologetic

   C resolute

   D apprehensive

13 The second stanza of the poem—

   A introduces the characters.

   B sets up the character's conflict.

   C gives away the ending.

   D explains the setting.

14 Which word from the passage is used to communicate a feeling of jealousy?

   A envying

   B chilling

   C killing

   D bringing

GO ON

15 What is the theme of this poem? Describe the images the speaker uses to convey this theme. Use examples from the poem to support your answer. (3 points)

_____

_____

_____

_____

_____

_____

_____

_____

_____

_____

Directions: Read the passage and answer the questions that follow.

Sonnet 18

by William Shakespeare

Shall I compare thee to a summer's day?
Thou art more lovely and more temperate:
Rough winds do shake the darling buds of May,
And summer's lease hath all too short a date:
Sometime too hot the eye of heaven shines,
And often is his gold complexion dimmed,
And every fair from fair sometime declines,
By chance, or nature's changing course untrimmed:
But thy eternal summer shall not fade,
Nor lose possession of that fair thou ow'st,
Nor shall death brag thou wand'rest in his shade,
When in eternal lines to time thou grow'st,
So long as men can breathe or eyes can see,
So long lives this, and this gives life to thee.

16 Finish the following word analogy.

ETERNAL : EVERLASTING :: Temperate :

    A extreme

    B moderate

    C passionate

    D peaceful

17 Compare the themes of "Annabel Lee" and "Sonnet 18." Then contrast their structure and styles. Use details from the poems to support your answer. (5 points)

_____

_____

_____

_____

_____

_____

_____

_____

_____

_____

_____

_____

_____

_____

_____

_____

Take a break. Then go on to Part 2.

Directions: Read the passage and answer the questions that follow.

from George Washington's Farewell Address (1796)

Against the insidious wiles of foreign influence (I conjure you to believe me, fellow-citizens) the jealousy of a free people ought to be constantly awake, since history and experience prove that foreign influence is one of the most baneful foes of republican government. But that jealousy to be useful must be impartial; else it becomes the instrument of the very influence to be avoided, instead of a defense against it. Excessive partiality for one foreign nation and excessive dislike of another cause those whom they actuate to see danger only on one side, and serve to veil and even second the arts of influence on the other. Real patriots who may resist the intrigues of the favorite are liable to become suspected and odious, while its tools and dupes usurp the applause and confidence of the people, to surrender their interests.

The great rule of conduct for us in regard to foreign nations is in extending our commercial relations, to have with them as little political connection as possible. So far as we have already formed engagements, let them be fulfilled with perfect good faith. Here let us stop. Europe has a set of primary interests which to us have none; or a very remote relation. Hence she must be engaged in frequent controversies, the causes of which are essentially foreign to our concerns. Hence, therefore, it must be unwise in us to implicate ourselves by artificial ties in the ordinary vicissitudes of her politics, or the ordinary combinations and collisions of her friendships or enmities.

Our detached and distant situation invites and enables us to pursue a different course. If we remain one people under an efficient government, the period is not far off when we may defy material injury from external annoyance; when we may take such an attitude as will cause the neutrality we may at any time resolve upon to be scrupulously respected; when belligerent nations, under the impossibility of making acquisitions upon us, will not lightly hazard the giving us provocation; when we may choose peace or war, as our interest, guided by justice, shall counsel.

Why forego the advantages of so peculiar a situation? Why quit our own to stand upon foreign ground? Why, by interweaving our destiny with that of any part of Europe, entangle our peace and prosperity in the toils of European ambition, rivalship, interest, humor or caprice?

It is our true policy to steer clear of permanent alliances with any portion of the foreign world; so far, I mean, as we are now at liberty to do it; for let me not be understood as capable of patronizing infidelity to existing engagements. I hold the maxim no less applicable to public than to private affairs, that honesty is always the best policy. I repeat it, therefore, let those engagements be observed in their genuine sense. But, in my opinion, it is unnecessary and would be unwise to extend them.

18 Which term best describes the structure of the passage?

   A least important to most important

   B cause and effect

   C chronological order

   D comparison and contrast

19 In the passage, the author's main argument is that—

   A trusting other countries' promises is advantageous.

   B aligning with other countries has risks.

   C being influenced by foreign powers is natural.

   D learning from other countries is necessary.

20 Based on the passage, which of the following does the author probably value most?

   A forming strong alliances

   B becoming part of Europe

   C maintaining neutrality

   D helping other countries

21 Which detail supports the idea that the author believes in honoring agreements?

   A So far as we have already formed engagements, let them be fulfilled with perfect good faith.

   B Our detached and distant situation invites and enables us to pursue a different course.

   C It is our true policy to steer clear of permanent alliances with any portion of the foreign world.

   D Why. . . entangle our peace and prosperity in the toils of European ambition?

22 What is the purpose of the questions in paragraph 4?

   A The questions outline how the author wants to change the current policy.

   B The questions describe the author's frustration with Europe.

   C The questions make a point in support of the author's argument.

   D The questions compare what happened in the past to what will happen in the future.

23 The word <u>alliances</u> in the last paragraph means—

   A a group of friends

   B a circle of acquaintances

   C an agreement among people

   D an association of nations

GO ON

Directions: Choose the best answer to complete the analogy.

24 INCREASE : REDUCTION :: partiality :

   A unity

   B loathing

   C admiration

   D simplification

Directions: Use the following dictionary entry to answer questions 25 and 26.

> **re-la-tion** (ri-ley-shuhn), [Latin *relatio*] *n.* 1. A connection between things, people, or countries. 2. A person connected to another person by blood or marriage. 3. A story narration. 4. An association between ordered pairs of numbers or objects as used in math.

25 Which definition best fits the use of the word <u>relations</u> in paragraph 2?

   A definition 1

   B definition 2

   C definition 3

   D definition 4

26 Which part of the dictionary entry explains the origin of the word?

   A re-la-tion

   B (ri-ley-shuhn)

   C [Latin *relatio*]

   D n.

from The Monroe Doctrine (1823)

James Monroe

It was stated at the commencement of the last session that a great effort was then making in Spain and Portugal to improve the condition of the people of those countries, and that it appeared to be conducted with extraordinary moderation. It need scarcely be remarked that the result has been so far very different from what was then anticipated. Of events in that quarter of the globe, with which we have so much intercourse and from which we derive our origin, we have always been anxious and interested spectators. The citizens of the United States cherish sentiments the most friendly in favor of the liberty and happiness of their fellow-men on that side of the Atlantic. In the wars of the European powers in matters relating to themselves we have never taken any part, nor does it comport with our policy so to do. It is only when our rights are invaded or seriously menaced that we resent injuries or make preparation for our defense. With the movements in this hemisphere we are of necessity more immediately connected, and by causes which must be obvious to all enlightened and impartial observers. The political system of the allied powers is essentially different in this respect from that of America. This difference proceeds from that which exists in their respective Governments; and to the defense of our own, which has been achieved by the loss of so much blood and treasure, and matured by the wisdom of their most enlightened citizens, and under which we have enjoyed unexampled felicity, this whole nation is devoted. We owe it, therefore, to candour and to the amicable relations existing between the United States and those powers to declare that we should consider any attempt on their part to extend their system to any portion of this hemisphere as dangerous to our peace and safety. With the existing colonies or dependencies of any European power we have not interfered and shall not interfere. But with the Governments who have declared their independence and maintained it, and whose independence we have, on great consideration and on just principles, acknowledged, we could not view any interposition for the purpose of oppressing them, or controlling in any other manner their destiny, by any European power in any other light than as the manifestation of an unfriendly disposition toward the United States. In the war between those new Governments and Spain we declared our neutrality at the time of their recognition, and to this we have adhered, and shall continue to adhere, provided no change shall occur which, in the judgment of the competent authorities of this Government, shall make a corresponding change on the part of the United States indispensable to their security.

The late events in Spain and Portugal shew that Europe is still unsettled. Of this important fact no stronger proof can be adduced than that the allied powers should have thought it proper, on any principle satisfactory to themselves, to have interposed by force in the internal concerns of Spain. To what extent such interposition may be carried, on the same principle, is a question in which all independent powers whose governments differ from theirs are interested, even those most remote, and surely none more so than the United States. Our policy in regard to Europe, which was adopted at an early stage of the wars which have so long agitated that quarter of the globe, nevertheless remains the same, which is, not to interfere in the internal concerns of any of its powers; to consider the government de facto as the legitimate government for us; to cultivate friendly relations with it, and to preserve those relations by a frank, firm, and manly policy, meeting in all instances the just claims of every power, submitting to injuries from none.

But in regard to those continents circumstances are eminently and conspicuously different. It is impossible that the allied powers should extend their political system to any portion of either continent without endangering our peace and happiness; nor can anyone believe that our southern brethren, if [left] to themselves, would adopt it of their own accord. It is equally impossible, therefore, that we should behold such interposition in any form with indifference. If we look to the comparative strength and resources of Spain and those new Governments, and their distance from each other, it must be obvious that she can never subdue them. It is still the true policy of the United States to leave the parties to themselves, in the hope that other powers will pursue the same course.

27 Based on the information in the first paragraph, what conclusion can you draw?

   A The United States will defend another nation's independence in certain cases.

   B The United States will refrain from interfering with any European disputes.

   C The United States will step in to stop the unrest in Spain and Portugal.

   D The United States will go to war to protect Spain.

28 Are the two presidential passages primary sources? Give reasons for your answer. (3 points)

_____

_____

_____

_____

_____

_____

_____

_____

_____

_____

_____

_____

_____

_____

29 Which of the following details from the passage is a fact?

    A Of events in that quarter of the globe, with which we have so much intercourse and from which we derive our origin, we have always been anxious and interested spectators.

    B The citizens of the United States cherish sentiments the most friendly in favor of the liberty and happiness of their fellow-men on that side of the Atlantic.

    C In the war between those new Governments and Spain we declared our neutrality at the time of their recognition.

    D It is impossible that the allied powers should extend their political system to any portion of either continent without endangering our peace and happiness.

30 Compare and contrast how the two passages address foreign policy. How do the passages recommend treating other nations? Support your answer with details from both passages. (3 points)

_____

_____

_____

_____

_____

_____

_____

_____

_____

_____

_____

_____

_____

Directions: Read the passage and answer the questions that follow.

from Moonbird: A Year on the Wind with the Great Survivor B95

by Phillip Hoose

In the next few months, from March to June, B95 and his flock mates will fly from the bottom of the world to the top-from the land of penguins to polar bear country. He will fly night and day, descending only to visit the regular fueling stations that have sustained him with protein all his life. He will arrive at each stop ravenously hungry, weighing much less than he did just days before. But if the food is there, and he can get to it, he will survive, refuel, and fly on.

B95 is a red knot of the subspecies rufa, a robin-size shorebird with streamlined wings that crook at the elbow and taper to a point. In northern spring and summer, his breast and much of his face are colored brilliant brick red, with reddish feathers sprinkled over his back. During the remainder of the year, his feathers change and his body becomes mostly gray and white.

B95's name—and fame—comes from the letter-and-number combination inscribed on an orange plastic flag fastened around his upper left leg. He is a perfectly formed male with a long bill and powerful chest. Throughout the course of his extraordinarily long life—about twenty years—scientists have captured and examined him four times, and observed him through binoculars and spotting scopes on dozens of other occasions. Because he is so old, and has survived so many difficult journeys, he has become the most celebrated shorebird in the world.

But trip by trip, B95 threads the sky with fewer companions. When he was first banded as a young bird in 1995, scientists estimated that there were about 150,000 rufa red knots in existence. Then, around the year 2000, these birds began dying by the thousands. Why? Evidence points to abrupt changes in the stopover sites along their Great Circuit, and even in the air through which they fly. A special challenge is the reduction of a very important source of food at Delaware Bay. B95's plight, and that of rufa red knots in general, poses one of the great conservation questions of recent years: Can humans and shorebirds coexist?

Answers will have to arrive soon, for now experts believe that fewer than 25,000 rufa red knots remain. That means that more than 80 percent of the population has disappeared just within B95's lifetime. This looming shadow of extinction makes B95's long life all the more improbable. Scientists ask themselves: How can this one bird keep going year after year when so many of his acquaintances drop from the sky or perish on the beaches?

B95's gritty success inspires action. A worldwide network of scientists, conservationists, researchers, students, and volunteers has sprung up to save rufa from extinction. Though they are stationed around the world, they team up to follow the knots as they migrate throughout the western hemisphere, communicating instantly with new, Web-based tools. They know they have their work cut out for them, but, like B95 himself, they are determined.

31 Which detail should be included in a summary of the passage?

A In the cooler months of the year, B95 has gray and white feathers.

B Fueling stations provide rufa red knots with food.

C Rufa red knots are nearing extinction.

D B95 has a long bill and a powerful chest.

32 Based on the passage, what inference can you make about rufa red knots?

A In time, developing bigger wing spans will allow them to fly further.

B They probably stop at the same places every year during their Great Circuit.

C Hunters have also played a role in their dwindling numbers.

D Male rufa red knots live longer than females.

33 What is one question the article answers by explaining how B95 has inspired people?

A What is being done to save rufas from extinction?

B How has B95 survived for so long?

C Why are rufas dying off so quickly?

D When will B95 be spotted next?

34 Which quotation from the article best reflects an inference that supports the answer to Number 33?

A *That means that more than 80 percent of the population has disappeared just within B95's lifetime.*

B *A special challenge is the reduction of a very important source of food at Delaware Bay.*

C *Evidence points to abrupt changes in the stopover sites along their Great Circuit, and even in the air through which they fly.*

D *They know they have their work cut out for them, but, like B95 himself, they are determined.*

35   Write a summary of the passage. Be sure to include only the main ideas. (3 points)

_____

_____

_____

_____

_____

_____

_____

_____

_____

_____

_____

_____

_____

_____

_____

Directions: Read the passage and answer the questions that follow.

from The Last Fish Tale

by Mark Kurlansky

New Englanders were not the only ones growing angry about foreign trawlers. As the vessels got larger and more menacing, and developed the capacity to go anywhere, it seemed most everyone was getting tired of "the foreigners" scooping up their fish. The Icelanders and the Norwegians were the first to propose exclusive national fishing zones. This was a reversal of international maritime law, which had always emphasized free access. In fact, denying access was often considered an act of war.

Iceland, long a backward, underdeveloped colony of Denmark, gained its independence in 1944 and wanted to base a new modern economy on fishing. But Icelandic waters had been a traditional British fishing ground, especially for cod and haddock, the favorite fish of the south of England and the latter the favorite of the north and Scots. The British had been fishing there since at least the fifteenth century. But once their stern trawlers started depleting the North Sea, British North Sea ports, especially Hull, became long-distance ports targeting Icelandic waters.

In 1950, when Iceland announced a 4-mile limit, the British, who had been claiming and enforcing exclusive fishing zones in the North Sea for centuries, were suddenly outraged by the concept. Eight years later, when Iceland extended the zone to twelve miles, the British were ready to go to war. There were three shooting wars—cod wars— in 1958, 1971–73, and 1975, all dangerous skirmishes between the British Royal Navy and the Icelandic Coast Guard. The Icelanders kept expanding their zone and the British kept resisting. But all the while, in its negotiations for entry into the European Common Market, Britain argued for its own zone of exclusion to keep out its European partners.

In truth, what was happening was that fishermen were gaining the ability to catch more fish than were available in the sea. During World War II, for six years, there had been almost no fishing in northern Europe. As a result, the fish stocks built up to levels that have never been seen since. But by the 1950s, catches around Iceland, in the North Sea, and even off Cornwall and around Ireland, the Irish box, were noticeably declining. There were two contradictory responses to this. Everyone wanted the foreigners out, but also everyone wanted to build up their own fishing capacity. The foreigners were not being thrown out to save the fish but, rather, so that the locals could catch more. As the local fleet caught more fish, fewer fish were available. The solution was to have more vessels that could travel farther with more power and larger nets. The problem with these responses, it can easily be seen now, but as was clear to only a few then, is that this creates a downward spiral. The new fleet would further deplete the stocks and the catch would be less, and so the fleet would forever have to be expanded to continue catching the same amount, resulting eventually in fewer fish and, finally, no fish at all.

In the 1970s, following Iceland's decision to declare a 200-mile exclusive fishing zone, most of the seagoing nations of the world did the same. For the United States, this was not a particularly difficult decision. In the country's early days, when it was little more than a dozen states concentrated along the Atlantic, and Massachusetts politicians such as Massachusetts native John Adams, a tireless supporter of New England fisheries, were leading figures, fishery issues were central to U.S. policy. But in modern times, such issues have been of concern to only a handful of the fifty states, and even Massachusetts leaders have rarely seen them as a priority. Of greater interest to Washington, a zone of exclusion had implications for mineral rights, for oil rights. In fact, to protect these rights, the United States had been fairly early in claiming its continental shelf, which by chance also includes the richest fishing grounds. By 1945 it was clear that parts of these shelves held valuable oil deposits, and then-president Harry Truman declared the United States the exclusive owner of the waters of its continental shelf, though the United States had not restricted access by foreign fishermen.

36 Which of the following claims supports the author's argument that fishermen were overfishing?

A *The British had been fishing there since at least the fifteenth century.*

B *Iceland . . . wanted to base a new modern economy on fishing.*

C *But by the 1950s, catches . . . were noticeably declining.*

D *. . . everyone wanted to build up their own fishing capacity.*

37 How do the various countries react to the idea of exclusive fishing zones in different ways? Use details and examples from the passage to support your answer. (5 points)

_____

_____

_____

_____

_____

_____

_____

_____

_____

_____

_____

_____

_____

_____

_____

_____

Take a break. Then go on to Part 3.

Directions: Read the passage and answer the questions that follow.

38 A participial phrase—

   A Can stand on its own as a sentence.

   B Includes a verbal and acts like an adjective.

   C Has a preposition plus a noun in it.

   D Begins with a relative pronoun.

39 All of the underlined parts of the following sentences are participial phrases EXCEPT—

   A <u>Leaping across the room</u>, she put out the fire quickly.

   B <u>After we ate the meal,</u> we pounced on a delicious chocolate pie.

   C The mysterious figure, <u>listening to the night</u>, paused, and then disappeared.

   D <u>His confidence shattered</u>, the professor tried to regain his composure.

40 Which of the following sentences has a relative clause?

   A Space travel would be an interesting experience, but it is not for everyone.

   B In 1969, Neil Armstrong became the first man to step onto the surface of the moon.

   C Buzz Aldrin, who was the second man to step onto the moon, is also an author.

   D Stepping onto the moon must have been a surreal experience for both astronauts.

41 Which of the following sentences has parallel structure?

   A Monty rushed to put on his coat, gloves, and don't forget his hat.

   B Monty's fingers, along with his arms, and body were frozen.

   C The weather station warned of dangerous roads and freezing temperatures.

   D Many vehicles slipped and are going into the ditch on the highway.

42 Which of the following sentences has a prepositional phrase?

   A Gina tried to think calmly and clearly.

   B She wondered where she had put the assignment.

   C Mrs. Stanton was not going to be happy.

   D Gina buried her head in her hands.

43 Rewrite the following sentence so that it has a dependent clause and an independent clause. (1 point)

Jackson came into the house.

_____

_____

44 Which sentence contains a dependent clause?

    A Darius is going to play basketball after he finishes his homework.

    B Working on homework can be so boring.

    C Some people might think that playing basketball is boring too.

    D Finishing homework is good for your mind, and playing basketball is good for your body.

45 Which sentence does NOT include misspelled words?

    A It is difficult to distinquish one twin from the other.

    B The video game included gorilla warfare.

    C Amber helped seperate and tally the votes.

    D It was a special celebration, so we were allowed to order dessert.

46 Which sentence is NOT punctuated correctly?

    A Wilbur is a sweetheart; he is the gentlest pet I have ever had.

    B Male lions get a lot of sleep; they can sleep for up to 20 hours a day.

    C Most books are interesting; this one, unfortunately, is not.

    D Music is a passion; and art is a passion too.

47 Which sentence uses correct capitalization?

    A Janie needs to meet Martin crane, the school counselor.

    B She wrote a great story called "An Embellished Life."

    C mr. crane wants Janie to enter a contest.

    D First prize wins $100 from the Hansen and dresden publishing Company.

48 Which sentence uses correct capitalization?

    A My Aunt is originally from China.

    B She came to portland, Oregon in 1999.

    C She is teaching me to speak Mandarin Chinese.

    D Her full name is xiao yu.

49 Which sentence does NOT include misspelled words?

    A Since the dawn of creattion, people have wanted more.

    B Mallory walked around with a dejekted air.

    C The prince's coronation is next week.

    D Please hand me the tellescope on that table.

50 Which of the following sentences does NOT use punctuation correctly?

    A I can't wait to do my favorite things: eating chocolate, getting a massage, and playing volleyball.

    B When we go rollerblading; we need to wear pads.

    C Hey, are you going to eat that, Tanya?

    D "Yes," Mrs. Perman said, "let's take a break."

Points Earned/Total = _____/70

Common Core
Grade
8

Keeping Score

	Points Earned / Total Points	Percent Score
Tryout Test	/70	%
Unit One Practice Test Reading Literature: Key Ideas and Details	/12	%
Unit Two Practice Test Reading Literature: Craft and Structure	/10	%
Unit Three Practice Test Reading Informational Text: Key Ideas and Details	/10	%
Unit Four Practice Test Reading Informational Text: Craft and Structure	/8	%
Unit Five Practice Test Reading Informational Text: Integration of Knowledge and Ideas	/12	%
Unit Six Practice Test Language: Conventions of Standard English	/10	%
Unit Seven Practice Test Language: Vocabulary	/10	%
Mastery Test	/70	%

1. Fill in the number of points you earned in the Points Earned box.

2. Use the Finding Percent chart on page 162 to figure out your Percent Score. Then fill in the % box.

3. Compare your Percent Scores for the Tryout Test and the Mastery Test. See how much you've learned!

Finding Percent

Number of Points on Test

8

1	2	3	4	5	6	7	8
13%	25%	38%	50%	63%	75%	88%	100%

10

1	2	3	4	5	6	7	8	9	10
10%	20%	30%	40%	50%	60%	70%	80%	90%	100%

12

1	2	3	4	5	6	7	8	9	10	11	12
8%	17%	25%	33%	42%	50%	58%	67%	75%	83%	92%	100%

70

1	2	3	4	5	6	7	8	9	10	11	12	13	14	15	16	17
1%	3%	4%	6%	7%	9%	10%	11%	13%	14%	16%	17%	19%	20%	21%	23%	24%

18	19	20	21	22	23	24	25	26	27	28	29	30	31	32	33	34
26%	27%	29%	30%	31%	33%	34%	36%	37%	39%	40%	41%	43%	44%	46%	47%	49%

35	36	37	38	39	40	41	42	43	44	45	46	47	48	49	50	51
50%	51%	53%	54%	56%	57%	59%	60%	61%	63%	64%	66%	67%	69%	70%	71%	73%

52	53	54	55	56	57	58	59	60	61	62	63	64	65	66	67	68
74%	76%	77%	79%	80%	81%	83%	84%	86%	87%	89%	90%	91%	93%	94%	96%	97%

69	70
99%	100%

WRITING TEST
WORKSHOPS

Writing Test Workshops

To the Student

Why Do I Need This Book?

This book will help you practice taking writing tests. You will learn how to—

- read a writing prompt.
- get your ideas down on paper.
- write to tell a story.
- write to explain.
- write about an opinion.

How Will My Writing Be Scored?

Your writing test will be scored by test readers who use rubrics, or scoring guides. The rubric below lists 6 qualities of good writing. Read through each characteristic so you know how your writing will be graded.

Rubric Score: *1* is the lowest; *5* is the highest					
Ideas/Content—focuses on one main idea; the details add to the main idea	①	②	③	④	⑤
Organization—has a clear beginning, middle, and end; the order is easy to follow	①	②	③	④	⑤
Voice—communicates feelings and personality; the writing is unique	①	②	③	④	⑤
Word Choice—uses colorful, fresh words in the right places	①	②	③	④	⑤
Sentence Fluency—uses both long and short sentences that flow smoothly	①	②	③	④	⑤
Conventions—has few or no spelling, capitalization, and punctuation errors	①	②	③	④	⑤

How to Manage Your Time During an Essay Test

You may have 20 to 45 minutes to complete a writing test, so it's important to have a plan.

If you have 20 minutes,

◎ read the prompt, circle key ideas, brainstorm, and organize ideas. (5 minutes)

◎ write the essay. (10 minutes)

◎ revise, edit, and proofread. (5 minutes)

How to Read a Writing Prompt

A *prompt* is the assignment for a writing test. The prompt gives you directions. It also tells you what to write about.

> ◎ **Step 1**
>
> Read through the entire prompt. Decide what the topic is.
>
> ◎ **Step 2**
>
> Read through the prompt a second time, underlining key words (*explain, compare, tell*) that will help you focus your writing.
>
> ◎ **Step 3**
>
> Look for key words or phrases you might use in your main idea statement.

Meera's Prompt

Here is a prompt for Meera's test. Look at the key ideas she underlined. These clues helped Meera understand what she is supposed to write about.

Prompt

Your principal is thinking about <u>requiring all ninth grade students to be involved in the school newspaper</u>. <u>The school newspaper is published once a month</u>. Decide how you feel about this idea. Write a paper in which you <u>present an argument</u> for or against such a requirement. Develop your argument by presenting claims <u>supported by reasons and facts.</u> Address at least <u>one counterclaim</u> in the paper.

The underlined words and phrases will guide Meera's essay. She will be writing a paper in which she must create an argument in support of or in opposition to a plan to require all ninth graders to be involved in the school newspaper. She must also address at least one counterclaim, or opposing claim.

Read the prompt below. Then underline the key words or phrases.

Prompt

Imagine that the curfew in your town is 9:00 p.m. every day. Explain whether this rule is fair. Describe your reasons for accepting the curfew as fair or for changing it because you don't think it is fair.

Argumentative Writing Tests

Argumentative Writing Tests

Review the Standards (W.9.1.a–e, W.9.4, W.9.5, WHST.9.1)
- Write **arguments** that support **claims**, using logical **reasons** and **relevant evidence**
- Introduce claims, acknowledge **opposing** claims, and present **counterclaims**
- Use **transitional words and phrases**
- Use a formal writing style
- Provide a concluding section

Some writing tests will ask you to write an **argument**. A good argument makes a **claim** (or claims) and then develops the claim with logical reasons and evidence such as facts and expert opinions.

Introduction
- establishes the topic
- states the claim(s)

  Claim: *Celebrities and professional athletes are paid too much.*

Body
- supports claim(s) with logical **reasons** and **relevant evidence**

  Reason: *Celebrities and athletes provide entertainment, not necessary services.*

  Evidence: *Police officers, who protect and save lives, are paid an average annual salary of $50,000, while celebrities and professional athletes may be paid millions.*

- acknowledges **opposing** claims and presents **counterclaims**

  Example: *Some argue that athletes and celebrities often have short careers and earn money for the team, the movie, or the show they are involved in, so they deserve their large paychecks. However, police officers risk their lives every day, and their careers may also be cut short—by a bullet or a deadly assault.*

- uses **transitional words and phrases** to show relationships between ideas (*however, on the other hand, likewise, in contrast*)
- maintains a formal style

Conclusion
- restates main claim(s)
- draws final conclusions based upon the argument

  Example: *In short, celebrities and professional athletes are indeed paid too much. When their salaries and duties are contrasted with the salaries and responsibilites of police officers, it is evident that entertainers are overpaid, while the brave men and women who protect and serve are not paid nearly enough.*

Max's Prompt

Below is a prompt Max was given on a writing test. Underline the key words in the prompt.

Prompt

Your school is considering cutting football from the sports program in response to new research that suggests a link between concussions and brain diseases later in life. Write a paper that develops an argument either for or against eliminating football from your school sports program. Support your claims with logical reasons and evidence. Address at least one opposing claim with a counterclaim.

Words used in opinion writing prompts

- Agree/disagree
- Argue/argument
- Convince
- Oppose
- Persuade
- Point of view/viewpoint
- Position
- Support

Before writing his paper, Max used a chart to help him organize his ideas.

Topic: <u>cutting football from the school sports program</u>

Claim: <u>Cutting program would prevent many athletes from getting hurt.</u>

Reasons for	Reasons against
Football is a full-contact sport that results in many injuries to young athletes.	The community would lose important events such as game nights and homecoming. **Counterclaim:** Other sports could fill the gap left by football and host more events.
Football has a culture where many athletes rejoin the game even after being injured.	Football teaches players to become part of a team and gives them a feeling of belonging. **Counterclaim:** Other sports such as basketball, volleyball, or soccer require teamwork and provide camaraderie.
Concussions are common in football but difficult to diagnose, and they can lead to headaches, memory loss, and other symptoms if not treated properly.	

GO ON

Read Max's paper. Then complete the tasks in the Looking at Max's Writing box.

Max's Writing

Football is a popular sport in America. Parents sign their children up and watch them play with their helmets thudding, shoulders angled for tackling, and bodies piling on top of one another after a fumble. Many don't realize how dangerous football can be. Cutting football from our schools sports roster would prevent many injuries to players.Also, the culture of warriors in football make players feel they should rush back into the game even after an injury. Concussions are common football-related injuries, but they are difficult to diagnose, even for doctors. One study indicated that 140,000 young football players receive concussions every year. Other sports have injuries, too, but football definitly leads in head-related injuries, which can lead to brain diseases later in life.It's true that important community events linked with football, such as homecoming and weakly games, would be eliminated if football were cut. The community would lose a time honored tradition of homecoming festivities as well as the weekly game nights at the football field. However, other sports could easily fill the gap left by football. Other sports could begin hosting a homecoming event. Or have a larger celebration. Community members can replace watching football with something else. Other sports that have felt

Looking at Max's Writing

- Locate Max's main idea. Then locate his supporting details. Cross out any details that do not support the main idea.

- Does the order of the reasons in the body make sense? Consider renumbering the paragraphs in the body to help build a stronger argument.

- Put a star by the opposing claim. Rewrite Max's counterclaim so that it is stronger.

- What can you tell about Max's personality from his writing style?

- Circle places you think Max might have used more lively verbs or precise nouns. Mark changes you would suggest.

- Mark and correct any errors in spelling, punctuation, capitalization, and grammar.

overshadowed by football could shine in the new spotlight.In short, football causes more head injuries than any other high school sport. These head injuries can have long term impacts on players, such as contributing to the development of head diseases. In addition, the warrior culture of football leads athletes to return to play after injury. Therefore, cutting football from the school's sports program would prevent many student athletes from getting hurt.

GO ON

Try It On Your Own

Now it's your turn to take a practice writing test. Follow the steps in order. If your teacher gives you a time limit, make a plan by filling in the number of minutes you have to complete each step.

Time Allowed

_____
minutes

Step 1—Read the prompt. Underline any key words and phrases. (_____ minutes)

Step 2—Brainstorm for some ideas on another piece of paper. (_____ minutes)

Step 3—Fill in the organizer with your ideas. (_____ minutes)

Prompt

Imagine that your state board of education is considering adding an art class to the high school curriculum. Students would have to take this class to graduate. How would you feel about such a change? Write a paper that develops an argument either for or against adding an art class to the high school curriculum. Develop a claim and support your claim with reasons and evidence. Be sure to include an opposing claim and counterclaim within your argument.

Topic: _____

Claim: _____
_____

Reasons for	Reasons against
	Counterclaim:
	Counterclaim:
	Counterclaim:

Step 4—Using your organizer as a guide, write your paper on a separate piece of paper. (_____ minutes)

Step 5—Go back and revise your paper. Then proofread your paper for mistakes in capitalization, punctuation, and grammar. (_____ minutes)

How Did You Do?

Now evaluate your own writing (or ask a friend to evaluate your writing). Complete the following tasks.

> **Consider This**
>
> 1. **Ideas/Content** Underline the central claim. Put a star by an opposing claim.
>   - Number the reasons that support your claim. Are the reasons supported with relevant evidence?
> 2. **Organization** Are the reasons organized logically? Yes _____ or No _____
>   - Put a box around linking words that show relationship between ideas: *however, likewise, in contrast.*
> 3. **Voice** Does the writer communicate a positive attitude or does he/she seem angry or sound like a know-it-all?
> 4. **Word Choice** Circle any words that seem especially fresh or vivid. Cross out any words that are not exciting or precise.
> 5. **Sentence Fluency** Put a check next to any sentences that seem too choppy, too long, or sound awkward. Are the sentences varied in length?
> 6. **Conventions** Check for any errors in spelling, capitalization, and punctuation.

Use your answers from the **Consider This** chart to help you fill in this rubric.

Rubric Score: *1* is the lowest; *5* is the highest					
Ideas/Content—focuses on one main idea; the details add to the main idea	①	②	③	④	⑤
Organization—has a clear beginning, middle, and end; the order is easy to follow	①	②	③	④	⑤
Voice—communicates feelings and personality; the writing is unique	①	②	③	④	⑤
Word Choice—uses colorful, fresh words in the right places	①	②	③	④	⑤
Sentence Fluency—uses both long and short sentences that flow smoothly	①	②	③	④	⑤
Conventions—has few or no spelling, capitalization, and punctuation errors	①	②	③	④	⑤

One way I can improve my writing is by _____

_____

Informative Writing Tests

Informative Writing

Review the Standards (W.9.2.a–f, W.9.4, W.9.5, WHST.9.2)

- Write **informative** texts
- Introduce a topic, previewing what is to follow
- Organize and develop the topic with relevant facts, definitions, and details
- Use **transitions** and precise language
- Use a formal style
- Provide a conclusion

When you write a paper comparing one baseball team to another or discussing the causes of World War I, you are writing to inform. Writing to inform is also called *expository writing*. **Informative** writing usually has the following three parts:

Introduction

- gets the reader's attention
- clearly presents the main idea:

Most high school students imagine going to college and getting a job as their set path for the future. However, a college education is becoming increasingly expensive due to a number of factors.

Body

- contains relevant, well-chosen facts, definitions, details, examples, and quotations (the more specific the better):

One reason for students paying more for college tuition is that the states are contributing less. In 1980, states paid about 1/2 of state college tuition costs, whereas in 2000, states only paid about 1/3 of the costs.

- is organized appropriately for the topic
- uses a variety of **transitions** appropriate to the organization (*most importantly, first, next, finally, in contrast*)
- uses precise language and specific words
- has a formal style, avoiding slang

Ways to Organize Information

- Compare and contrast—All the differences, then all the similarities or by details
- Chronologically—Events or steps in time order
- Logically—Least to most important facts or details

Conclusion

- follows logically from the ideas presented in the body
- ends with a strong thought:

Overall, students can expect the trend of increasingly expensive college tuition to continue.

Mariah's Prompt

Below is an example of an expository prompt that Mariah was given on a writing test.

Help her out by underlining the important ideas.

Everyone has a favorite hobby or pastime. Tell what you like to do the best. Explain why you enjoy this activity.

Before writing her paper, Mariah used an idea web to help her organize her ideas.

Words used in informative writing prompts

- Compare/contrast
- Define
- Explain
- Summarize
- Tell

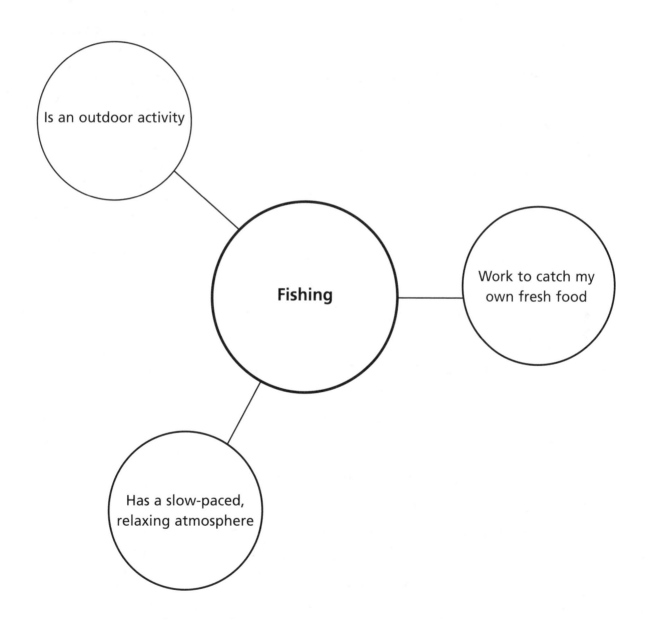

Is an outdoor activity

Fishing

Work to catch my own fresh food

Has a slow-paced, relaxing atmosphere

GO ON

Read Mariah's paper. Then complete the tasks in the Looking at Mariah's Writing box.

Mariah's Writing

Fishing is a favorite pastime in the United States. In fact, about 16 percent of Americans went fishing in 2001. These Americans have realized what I already know: fishing is a great recreational activity.

First of all, fishing is relaxing. Once the tackle box is ready and the bait fresh, setting out to fish is a slow-paced adventure. Imagine resting on a blanket on the soft bank of a river with your rod and reel next to you. Time passes lazily until a fish nibbles on the bait, and then excitement ensues while the fish is reeled in and placed in the bucket. Once the brief thrill of the catch is over, the day peacefully drifts along again with no worries or cares intruding.

Being outdoors lends another layer to the relaxing atmosphere. A low stress atmosphere is a rarity in these times when productivity and keeping busy seem to be the most important things. The chance to unwind in the great outdoors comes hand in hand with fishing.

Along with reducing stress, fishing offers another health benefit. Exposure to the sun's UVB rays helps the body receive the vitamin D it needs. According to the Mayo Clinic, "vitamin D deficiency is more common than previously thought." So while sunscreen is still recommended, absorbing some of the sun's rays during fishing is good for health.

Looking at Mariah's Writing

- Label Mariah's main idea statement with an **M**. Label her supporting details with an **S**.
- Look for the following elements of structure: a clear beginning, middle, and end; topic sentences; transitions.
- What does Mariah's writing style reveal about her personality?
- Circle any lively verbs or precise nouns Mariah uses.
- Locate sentences that don't flow well. Suggest ways to fix them.
- Correct any spelling, capitalization, punctuation, or grammatical errors in Mariah's writing.

Nowadays, people focus on eating healthy and eating organic, yet many don't want to grow or catch their own food. Fishing is easy to learn. It is fairly inexpensive too. Catching one's own meal can be quite satisfying. Eating fish that was just caught guarantees its freshness, and of course, fish is a low fat food to begin with.

In conclusion, fishing is an enjoyable pastime that provides several health benefits. A relaxing atmosphere lowers stress levels, and exposure to sunlight gives the body vitamin D. Catching one's own fish is an exciting adventure. Lastly, no matter how it is cooked, nothing can beat the taste of freshly caught fish.

GO ON

Try It On Your Own

Directions: Now it's your turn to take a practice writing test. Follow the steps in order. If your teacher gives you a time limit, make a plan by filling in the number of minutes you have to complete each step.

_____ minutes

Step 1—Read the prompt below and underline any key words and phrases. (_____ minutes)

Step 2—Brainstorm for some ideas on another piece of paper. (_____ minutes)

Step 3—Fill in the idea web with your ideas. (_____ minutes)

Prompt

At this point, you have survived the transition from middle school to high school. No doubt younger students could benefit from your experience. Write a paper that explains how to survive the first year of high school. Support your ideas with plenty of examples. Keep in mind that you are writing for students at approximately the eighth-grade level.

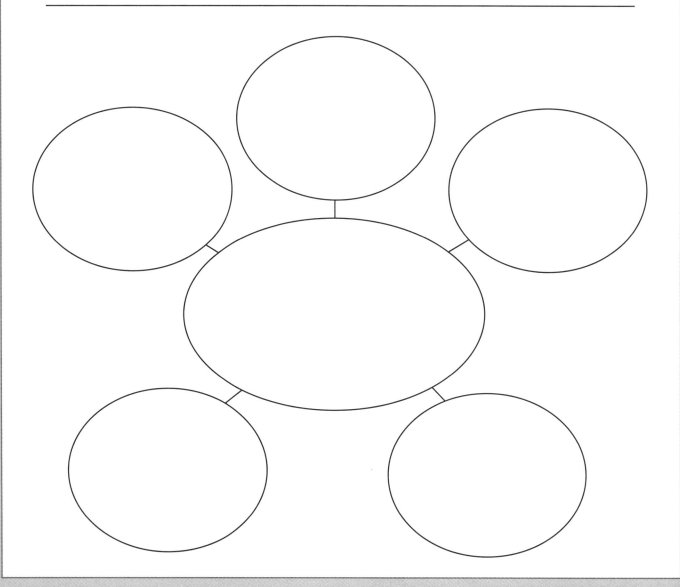

Step 4—Using your idea web as a guide, write your essay on a separate piece of paper. (_____ minutes)

Step 5—Go back and revise your paper. Then proofread your paper for mistakes in capitalization, punctuation, and grammar. (_____ minutes)

How Did You Do?

Now evaluate your own writing (or ask a friend to evaluate your paper). Complete the following tasks.

Consider This

1. **Ideas/Content** Underline the main idea.
   - Number the supporting details that support the main idea. (1, 2, 3, etc.)
2. **Organization** Are the supporting points arranged logically? Yes _____ or No _____
   - Put a box around linking words such as *first*, *next*, *second*, *finally*, and *also*.
3. **Voice** Put a **V** next to any part of the story where the writer's voice doesn't fit the topic or seems strange.
4. **Word Choice** Circle any words that seem especially fresh or vivid. Cross out any words that are boring or not precise.
5. **Sentence Fluency** Put a check next to any sentences that seem too choppy or too long.
6. **Conventions** Check for any errors in spelling, capitalization, and punctuation.

Use your answers from the **Consider This** chart to help you fill in this rubric.

Rubric Score: *1* is the lowest; *5* is the highest					
Ideas/Content—focuses on one main idea; the details add to the main idea	①	②	③	④	⑤
Organization—has a clear beginning, middle, and end; the order is easy to follow	①	②	③	④	⑤
Voice—communicates feelings and personality; the writing is unique	①	②	③	④	⑤
Word Choice—uses colorful, fresh words in the right places	①	②	③	④	⑤
Sentence Fluency—uses both long and short sentences that flow smoothly	①	②	③	④	⑤
Conventions—has few or no spelling, capitalization, and punctuation errors	①	②	③	④	⑤

I can improve my writing _____

_____

Narrative
Writing
Tests

Narrative Writing

Review the Standards (W.9.3.a–e, W.9.4, W.9.5)

- Write **narratives** to develop real or imagined experiences
- Introduce a **context**, **point of view**, **characters**, and/or **narrator**
- Use **dialogue**, **pacing**, and **description**
- Use **transition** words and phrases, precise words, relevant descriptive details, and **sensory** language
- Provide a conclusion

When you tell your friends about something you did during winter break or write a tall tale, you are narrating events. Good **narratives** have three parts:

Beginning

- engages the readers with an interesting **context** (setting)
- establishes a **point of view** (Use first person to tell your own story. Use third person if an outside narrator is telling the events.)
- introduces the **characters**
- may include a main idea statement:

The worst day of my life was the day I met Cassidy Stevens.

Middle

- presents events (rising action) that build to a climax
- uses transition words and phrases (*first, later, a few days after that*)
- uses **description**, **sensory language**, and **dialogue**
- has good **pacing**

Dialogue brings characters to life and keeps the pace moving.

Instead of writing, *My friend Cassidy glanced out the window in surprise,* write,
"Hey, did you see that?" Cassidy asked anxiously as she glanced out the window.

Ending/Conclusion

- resolves the conflict
- may reflect on the significance of the events:

Even though I was covered in leaves, spider webs, and maybe a little bit of barbecue sauce, I realized that I wouldn't change a thing.

Pacing means how fast or slow the story moves. Use description and longer sentences to slow down the pace. Use dialogue and shorter sentences to pick up the pace.

José's Prompt

Below is a prompt José was given on a writing test. Underline the key words in the prompt.

Prompt

Most people have a memory that they treasure: a vacation, a time they spent with a relative, a celebration, or a new experience. Tell the story of one of your most treasured memories. Where were you? What were you doing? What makes it so special to you? Describe the memory in detail so readers gain an appreciation for it.

Before beginning to write his narrative, José used the following chart to help him organize the events he wanted to write about.

Topic: most treasured memory
Main idea: when I went to India
Event 1: the flight
Event 2: the taxi
Event 3: the Taj Mahal
Climax: walking in the Taj Mahal
Conclusion: looking at the photos reminds me how much fun I had in India

Read José's paper. Then complete the tasks in the Looking at José's Writing box.

José's Writing

My most treasured memory is the time I went to India. My parents and I were finally taking a family vacation, and we decided to go all the way to India. I didn't know what to expect, but it turned out to be an awesome trip.

The flight to India took about 20 hours total. It was made up of two long flights and a couple of shorter ones. I sat next to an interesting lady named Priya. She was a college student who lived in Chicago, and she was going back to visit her family in Bangalore. She was studying to be a doctor and lived with two other students in an apartment.

"Are you nervous about going to India?" Priya asked.

I gulped and replied, "Yeah, I mean, I don't even speak the language!"

Priya laughed, "Don't worry about that. Most Indians speak a fair amount of English, and anyway, India has maybe 13 official languages, so it would be rather difficult for you to learn them all."

My eyes almost bulged out of my head as I blurted out, "13 languages? Do you know them all?"

Shaking her head, Priya said, "Oh, no, I only speak three languages: English, Hindi, and Kannada."

Wow, I thought, she acts like speaking three languages is no big deal.

Fnally, we landed at the airport. I waved goodbye to Priya, and my family and I headed out the doors to find a taxi to take us to the hotel.

Looking at José's Writing

- What is the main idea of José's story?
- Locate the transitional words and phrases José uses.
- Circle any details that are not relevant, or meaningful, to the story.
- Examine the sentences that reveal details about José's trip. Does he reveal these details mostly through dialogue or description? What additional details might he have included?

We squeezed our luggage and ourselves into the taxi cab, and we were suddenly on our way. The streets were filled with vehicles of all sizes, including motorcycles, auto rickshaws, big trucks, and cars. The air was filled with the smell of exhaust. Our ears were constantly bombarded with the sound of honking horns. I noticed a phrase that was often painted on the back of the big trucks, "Horn OK." I asked my dad about it, and he said that traffic over here doesn't really follow the rules like in the U.S., so horn honking announced that someone was coming or going or changing lanes.

After we fell exhausted and jet lagged into our comfy hotel beds, we arose refreshed and ready to start our touring activities. First on our list was the Taj Mahal, probably the most famous Indian monument. I'll never forget my first sight of it with its exquisite white marble and its immense presence. It was huge. I thought nothing could be more beautiful until I saw an image of the Taj Mahal in the vast reflecting pool. It looked like another Taj Mahal had been built until tiny ripples disturbed the image in the pool. We wandered around the enormous mausoleum and the gardens for hours.

"All right, time to go," my mom announced with a tired smile.

"Okay," I replied as I gazed around the site one last time. I wanted to drink in everything about this moment.

The flight back home was just as long as the way there, but we were exhausted and slept most of the way. All of the wonderful sights and incredible experiences are now just memories. Whenever I look at the fabulous photos we took, I remember my trip of a lifetime.

Try It On Your Own

Directions: Now it's your turn to take a practice writing test. Follow the steps in order. If your teacher gives you a time limit, make a plan by filling in the number of minutes you have to complete each step.

Time Allowed

_____
minutes

Step 1—Read the prompt and underline any key words or phrases. (_____ minutes)

Step 2—Brainstorm for some ideas on another piece of paper. (_____ minutes)

Step 3—Fill in the organizer with your ideas. (_____ minutes)

Prompt

Everyone needs help sometimes. Tell the story of a time when you needed help. Who helped you? Why did you need help? How did that person help you? Describe the event in detail.

Topic:
Main idea:
Event 1:
Event 2:
Event 3:
Climax:
Conclusion:

Step 4—Using your graphic organizer as a guide, write your essay on a separate piece of paper. (_____ minutes)

Step 5—Go back and revise your paper. Then proofread your paper for mistakes in capitalization, punctuation, and grammar. (_____ minutes)

How Did You Do?

Now evaluate your own writing (or ask a friend to evaluate your writing).

Consider This

1. **Ideas/Content** Underline the main idea.
   - Can you identify the setting and the main characters?
   - Write a **D** next to examples of good dialogue and description.
2. **Organization** Is the order of events easy to follow?
   - Place a **B** in the margin next to the beginning, or introduction.
   - Place an **M** in the margin next to the middle.
   - Place an **E** in the margin next to the ending.
3. **Voice** Put a **V** next to a section where the writer's personality shines through the writing.
4. **Word Choice** Circle three examples of sensory language. If you can't find three examples, look for places where words that appeal to the senses could be inserted.
5. **Sentence Fluency** Put a box around a section of the writing where both long and short sentences fit together smoothly. Write FLOW next to any sentences that seem too choppy.
6. **Conventions** Put a checkmark above any errors in spelling, capitalization, or punctuation.

Use your answers from the **Consider This** chart to help you fill in this rubric.

Rubric Score: *1* is the lowest; *5* is the highest					
Ideas/Content—focuses on one main idea; the details add to the main idea	①	②	③	④	⑤
Organization—has a clear beginning, middle, and end; the order is easy to follow	①	②	③	④	⑤
Voice—communicates feelings and personality; the writing is unique	①	②	③	④	⑤
Word Choice—uses colorful, fresh words in the right places	①	②	③	④	⑤
Sentence Fluency—uses both long and short sentences that flow smoothly	①	②	③	④	⑤
Conventions—has few or no spelling, capitalization, and punctuation errors	①	②	③	④	⑤

I can improve my writing by _____

_____

Research Writing Tests

Research Report Writing

Review the Standards (W.9.4, W.9.5, W.9.7, W.9.8, WHST.9.7, WHST.9.8, WHST.9.9)

- Conduct short research projects to answer a question
- Draw on several sources
- Draw evidence from informational texts to support analysis and research

Sometimes a writing test or performance task will require you to conduct research and then write a research report. These types of testing events may take place over several days. You will be given time to go to the media center or computer lab.

A research report is organized much like an informational or argumentative essay.

Introduction
- gets the reader's attention
- contains the main idea

Body
- gives details that support the main idea
- contains good transitional words and phrases

Conclusion
- restates the main idea
- summarizes supporting details
- ends with a strong thought

Aisha's Prompt
Below is a prompt given to Aisha by her science teacher. Notice the main ideas she underlined.

Prompt

Conduct research on the "seasonal flu," an upper respiratory system viral infection and its vaccine. Explore the symptoms and the vaccine. Gather information from four different sources. Organize your notes into a written report in which you include information from all four sources.

Evaluating Sources

Use the following questions to evaluate a source.

Are the writers experts or authorities on the subject? Does the author of the article or book have an advanced degree or has she spent many years studying the subject? Web addresses that end in .gov or .edu indicate that the source is from a government agency or educational body that usually has greater authority.

Who is behind it? Is the source from a business or group that has a reason for promoting some information and withholding other facts?

When was it written? The information must be up-to-date. Remember that some topics (medical research, technology) are changing rapidly so you must use the most recent sources.

Aisha turned the important ideas from the writing prompt into questions to guide her research. As she conducted her research, Aisha kept careful notes, including where she found her information. Below is a sample of her notes.

When is the flu season?

—The flu season varies from year to year, but it is usually from October to mid-May. Flu season typically experiences a peak in January or February. (Johnson, Dana. "Prevent the Flu by Getting Vaccine." Wisconsin State Journal. 02 Oct. 2013: C2.eLibrary. Web. 29 Jan. 2014.)

—"Over a period of 31 seasons between 1976 and 2007, estimates of flu-associated deaths in the United States range from a low of about 3,000 to a high of about 49,000. During a regular flu season, about 90 percent of deaths occur in people 65 years and older." (www.cdc.gov)

What are the types of influenza?

—The two main types of the flu are Influenza A and Influenza B.

—"Influenza A viruses can be broken down into sub-types depending on the genes that make up the surface proteins. Over the course of a flu season, different types (A & B) and sub-types (influenza A) of influenza circulate and cause illness." (www.cdc.gov)

Avoiding Plagiarism

Plagiarism is copying a passage directly from a book and using it in your paper without giving credit to the writer. Avoid plagiarism by paraphrasing, or putting information in your own words. As you take notes from your sources, be sure to put quotation marks around any passages you copy directly from the source. This will help you identify which information is in your own words and which is a direct quotation. Notice which of Aisha's notes are direct quotations.

GO ON

—"In 1918 at the end of World War I, "Spanish Flu" infected one-fifth of the people in the world, killing more than 20 million, almost twice as many as perished in the war. A primitive vaccine proved useless as that outbreak and its milder 1919 variant attacked 28 percent of Americans and carried off 500,000, one-half of 1 percent of the U.S. population. No outbreak since has approached such dire proportions, yet influenza can still be deadly. Every year 10,000 to 20,000 Americans die from its complications, with up to 40,000 mortalities in years when new influenza strains appear." (Ackerman, S.J.. "Flu Shots; Do You Need One? Every Year 10,000 to 20,000 Americans Die from the Complications of Flu." FDA Consumer. 01 Oct. 1989: 8(4). eLibrary. Web. 29 Jan. 2014.)

—The flu virus changes over time, so another outbreak of the "Spanish Flu" is not likely (Ackerman.)

What are symptoms of the flu?

—"While small children can have vomiting and diarrhea with influenza, when most people say they have the "stomach flu," the illness they have is caused by a virus, not influenza" (Johnson).

—symptoms include fever or chills, feeling feverish, cough, sore throat, body aches, muscle aches, fatigue, runny or stuffy nose, or headaches. (www.cdc.gov)

How does the vaccine work?

—every year officials pick three influenza virus strains to include in the vaccine. The effectiveness of the vaccine varies depending on whether the strains included in it match the strains found during flu season. ("Public Health Infrastructure's Flu Response." Federal Document Clearing House, 10 Feb. 2004.eLibrary. Web. 29 Jan. 2014.)

—80% of vaccinated people are protected, and those who get the flu usually have milder symptoms than those who are not vaccinated ("Public Health").robonaut.html)

—"The first effective influenza vaccine was derived in 1943 and administered to U.S. military forces during World War II. No major flu outbreak occurred, despite wartime conditions ideal for the spread of the disease" (Ackerman).

Who should get the vaccine?

—"infants, the elderly (even some without obvious underlying health problems), and people plagued with chronic heart and lung ailments"("Influenza; CDC Says Vaccination Now is Best Protection Against Slow-Starting Flu Season." TB & Outbreaks Weekly. 16 Jan. 2001: 1516.eLibrary. Web. 29 Jan. 2014.)

—"Very few people should not be vaccinated with inactivated influenza vaccine: those with strong egg allergies, those with high fevers at the time the injection is to be given, and anyone with a previous severe adverse reaction to influenza vaccine" (Ackerman).

GO ON

From her notes, Aisha created an outline. This helped her organize her ideas before she wrote her paper.

Main Idea

Scientists develop vaccines to combat Influenza A and B, the viruses that affect people during the flu season.

I. What is flu season?
   A. When strains of Influenza A and Influenza B circulate
   B. Flu season is from October to mid-May
   C. "Spanish Flu"
   D. Certain groups are more at risk and should get the vaccine

II. What are the symptoms of the flu?
   A. List of symptoms
   B. Influenza versus stomach flu

III. How effective is the vaccine?
   A. First effective influenza vaccine was used on soldiers
   B. Officials choose three strains to put in the vaccine
   C. 80% of vaccinated people are protected

Looking at Aisha's Writing

Find and underline Aisha's main idea statement.

Does the introduction get your attention?
Yes _____ No _____

Does the order make sense?
Yes _____ No _____

Circle any transitional words or phrases.

Does she meet the requirement of using at least four sources?
Yes _____ No _____

Cross out any sentences that stray from the main idea of the paragraph.

Read Aisha's paper and answer the questions in the Looking at Aisha's Writing boxes.

Understanding the Flu

Flu season comes every year and affects most Americans, yet many do not realize just how serious the flu can be. In fact, it can be deadly. That makes the vaccine important, and scientists work on developing an effective flu vaccine every year.

First of all, flu season occurs when Influenza A and Influenza B are circulated throughout the population. "Influenza A viruses can be broken down into sub-types depending on the genes that make up the surface proteins," but Influenza B is categorized by strains ("Seasonal Influenza"). Flu season varies from year to year, but it is usually from October to mid-May. Flu season typically experiences a peak in January or February (Johnson).

In 1918, the "Spanish Flu" infected 2 percent of the world's population. It killed more than 20 million people. That is more than the number of soldiers killed in World War I. A vaccine developed at the time did not help, but no flu outbreak since that time has been so lethal. Nevertheless, the "Spanish Flu" proves what many may not realize: the flu can be deadly. In fact, "Every year 10,000 to 20,000 Americans die from its complications, with up to 40,000 mortalities in years when new influenza strains appear" (Ackerman). However, because the flu virus changes over time, another outbreak of the "Spanish Flu" will probably not happen.

Looking at Aisha's Writing

Are there any times Aisha plagiarized information? Write **Needs Citation** next to any passages where the source should be cited.

Does she use standard English and avoid using slang or informal language? Cross out any slang.

Mark and correct any problems in spelling, capitalization, punctuation, and grammar.

GO ON

Certain groups of people are more at risk for suffering complications from the flu and should get the vaccine. These people include babies, the elderly, and those who have heart and lung problems ("Influenza"). The elderly are particularly at risk. "During a regular flu season, about 90 percent of deaths occur in people 65 years and older" ("Seasonal Influenza").

A few groups of people should not receive the flu vaccine. Those with a severe allergy to eggs, a high fever when they are about to be vaccinated, and a severe adverse reaction to a previous flu vaccination should not be vaccinated. (Ackerman).

The stomach flu is different from influenza although people commonly mix up the two. Symptoms of the flu, or influenza, include fever or chills, feeling feverish, cough, sore throat, body aches, muscle aches, fatigue, runny or stuffy nose, or headaches ("Seasonal Influenza"). Usually only small children can experience the vomiting and diarrhea that make some people confuse the stomach flu with influenza (Johnson).

In 1943, the first effective influenza vaccine was given to soldiers during World War II. Even though wartime conditions make it easy for the flu to circulate, a major outbreak didn't happen (Ackerman).

Every year scientists work to predict which flu strain will impact people, and officials pick three influenza virus strains to include in the vaccine. The effectiveness of the vaccine varies depending on whether the strains included in it match the strains found during flu season. 80% of vaccinated people are protected, and those who get the flu usually have milder symptoms than those who are not vaccinated ("Public Health").

In short, the flu season comes and goes every year, while scientists work on developing effective vaccines to combat it. History has shown that influenza can be a dangerous virus, so the development of an effective vaccine is important.

Works Cited

"Influenza; CDC Says Vaccination Now is Best Protection Against Slow- Starting Flu Season." TB & Outbreaks Weekly. 16 Jan. 2001: 1516. eLibrary. Web. 29 Jan. 2014.

Johnson, Dana. "Prevent the Flu by Getting Vaccine." Wisconsin State Journal. 02 Oct. 2013: C2. eLibrary. Web. 29 Jan. 2014.

"Public Health Infrastructure's Flu Response." Federal Document Clearing House, 10 Feb. 2004.eLibrary. Web. 29 Jan. 2014.

"Seasonal Influenza (Flu)." Center for Disease Control and Prevention. 15 Jan. 2014. Web. 29 Jan. 2014.

GO ON

Try It On Your Own

Step 1—Read the prompt below. Then underline key words and phrases.

Prompt

Your world history class has been learning about Encland. Research Hadrian's Wall. Write a report explaining the history of the wall, including how and why it was built. Include information from at least four different sources.

Step 2—Turn the information from the prompt into questions to guide your research. Write your question(s) below.

_____

_____

_____

_____

_____

_____

_____

_____

_____

_____

_____

Step 3—Conduct research to answer the questions(s). Be sure to use the guidelines given in the prompt. Keep your research organized by including the source information next to your notes.

Step 4—Create an outline with your main idea and supporting details.

Main Idea

_____

_____

I. _____

_____

_____

_____

_____

_____

II. _____

_____

_____

_____

_____

_____

_____

III. _____

_____

_____

_____

_____

_____

_____

Step 5—Using your outline as a guide, write your report on a separate piece of paper. Be sure to cite your sources when you use them in your paper.

Step 6—Go back and proofread your paper for mistakes in capitalization, punctuation, and grammar.

How Did You Do?

Now evaluate your own writing (or ask a friend to evaluate your writing). Complete the following tasks.

Consider This

1. **Ideas/Content** Underline the main idea.
   - Number the details that support the main idea. (1, 2, 3, etc.)
   - Does the report meet the requirements of the prompt? Yes ____ No ____
   - Does the paper include information from at least four sources? Yes ____ No ____
   - Write **Needs Citation** next to any passages that are missing a citation.
2. **Organization** Can you identify the introduction and conclusion? Write **I** and **C** next to them.
   - Put a box around transitional words such as *first*, *next*, *second*, *finally*, and *also*.
3. **Voice** Does the writing communicate a confident, formal voice? Yes ____ No ____
4. **Word Choice** Circle any words that seem especially fresh or vivid.
   - Cross out any slang or words too informal for a research report.
5. **Sentence Fluency** Put a check next to any sentences that seem too choppy or too long.
6. **Conventions** Are quotation marks used with direct quotations? Yes ____ No ____
   - Check for any errors in spelling, capitalization, and punctuation.

Use your answers from the **Consider This** chart to help you fill in this rubric.

Rubric Score: *1* is the lowest; *5* is the highest					
Ideas/Content—focuses on one main idea; the details add to the main idea; appropriate sources are used	①	②	③	④	⑤
Organization—has a clear beginning, middle, and end; the order is easy to follow	①	②	③	④	⑤
Voice—communicates feelings and personality; the writing is unique	①	②	③	④	⑤
Word Choice—uses colorful, fresh words in the right places	①	②	③	④	⑤
Sentence Fluency—uses both long and short sentences that flow smoothly	①	②	③	④	⑤
Conventions—has few or no spelling, capitalization, and punctuation errors	①	②	③	④	⑤

One way I can improve my writing is by _____

_____

_____